Out

Out of Order

Tony Banks
and Jo-Ann Goodwin

Century · London

First published 1993
© Tony Banks and Jo-Ann Goodwin 1993

First published in the United Kingdom in 1993 by
Century Limited
Random House, 20 Vauxhall Bridge Road, London SW1V 2SA

Random House Australia (Pty) Limited
20 Alfred Street, Milsons Point, Sydney,
New South Wales 2061, Australia

Random House New Zealand Limited
18 Poland Road, Glenfield
Auckland 10, New Zealand

Random House South Africa (Pty) Limited
PO BOX 337, Bergvlei, South Africa

Random House UK Limited Reg. No. 954009

ISBN 0 7126 5840 8

Filmset by SX Composing Ltd, Rayleigh, Essex
Printed by Clays Ltd, St Ives plc

To our Dads

Contents

Acknowledgements

We would like to thank the following people for being kind enough to assist in the preparation of this book by giving their help and advice: Angela Beveridge, Ed Boyle, David Clark, Jeanette Gould, John Goodwin, Jerry Hayes MP, the Rt Hon. Neil Kinnock MP, Hugh McKinney, Robert McGeachy, Peter Mandelson MP, John Reid MP, Andrew Ridley, the House of Commons library staff and Labour Party research staff in the House of Commons and Walworth Road. We would also like to make it very clear that none of those mentioned are in any way implicated in what is to follow. The responsibility for the proffered interpretation and explanation of life in the House of Commons rests with the authors.

Introduction

Occasionally a book produced by an MP will stand out like a beacon, so powerful it becomes a work of scholarship. Not unsurprisingly, this work is not in that category. No one gets literary genius for £6.99 these days. This modest offering merely sets out to provide a slightly quirky look at the workings of Westminster.

Politicians love writing books, almost as much as they love making speeches. Some of those books have provided valuable insights as to the workings of government. A glimpse into the minds of those we elect, usually more in hope than expectation. Often the book is intended for posterity. To give history a gentle steer towards a more favourable impression of the author. This is no bad thing, given that most politicians, in terms of their character and intentions, are interpreted for us, and usually by those whose own motives are worthy of much closer investigation. Then, of course, there is the wholly shameless exercise of rewriting history completely. Everything the politician failed to achieve in office is accomplished or excused in a book, written with the luxury of hindsight before the event.

Being an MP is something special, but MPs themselves are nothing special. Anyone could do the job, and it's rather a pity that far more people aren't given a crack at it. Perhaps Westminster should be run on the same basis as the jury system, with all qualifying citizens eventually getting the call. What so often happens at present, is that the self-same MP who was very grateful to be elected in the first instance soon gets to believe it's a birthright. A disturbingly large number of what once were slightly overawed newcomers can quickly be seen strutting their stuff around Westminster's neo-gothic lobbies, as to the manner born.

Anyone remotely familiar with political activity knows the type. The self-satisfied jerk who keeps you waiting for an eternity in the Central Lobby, and then cuts you off mid-sentence to greet someone else considered far more important. Perhaps you've had the excruciating experience of standing behind one of these creatures in an airline queue? It's flesh-creepingly embarrassing. Only a person entirely devoid of all shame and sensitivity would start banging on about being an MP and well known to the Chairman of British Airways, all in the cause of getting a free first-class ticket upgrade.

Dear Reader, don't take all this lying down. The pompous piece of suiting who patronises you at Westminster is the self-same creep who came knocking on your door in the last Election, wearing a ridiculously large rosette, an oily grin, and begging for your vote.

Of course, they're not all equally awful. Statistically it would be impossible to get six hundred and fifty identikit MPs, given the many and various political routes that lead to Westminster. Truth to say, MPs are a fair cross-section of society, not in terms of gender or ethnic background, but rather by embodying all the characteristics that make up the human psyche. All human life is there, and quite a lot of low-life to boot.

If you detect a streak of cynicism in this book, then blame it on the system. The British political process has an inbuilt tendency to convert idealism into careerism, to turn radical meat into bourgeois sausage. Over the years no end of barricade-stormers have been enveloped and politically lobotomised by the sweet, cloying embrace of Westminster.

The fault in all this often lies not so much with the individual MP, as with the demands made of him or her. The workload alone can break the political will or physical strength of the most stakhanovite member. Those who refuse to compromise are made to suffer. The Tony Benns and Dennis Skinners are merely the exceptions that prove the rule.

In the end perhaps we are all guilty: the electorate for expecting far too much from their representatives, and they in their turn for promising far more than they have the ability to deliver. In recent years this has led to a tension between electors and elected that has become dangerous for the democratic process itself. Mutual mistrust, at times mutual contempt.

This book ventures no opinion on such profound developments, but instead offers a rough guide to the opportunities and pitfalls that both the well-intentioned and the self-serving should be aware of in their quest for power.

To help us on our journey, we have made reference to the various dilemmas which faced Stan Bonky MP as he set out to climb the greasy pole. Throughout his political life, Stan was a man who believed that ethics was a county east of London. No one could be better qualified to lead us through the maze.

Tony Banks
Jo-Ann Goodwin

Chapter One

How to Get to Westminster

So, attracted by visions of fame and glory, of righting wrongs, fighting injustice, going on fact-finding trips to sunny places, and getting on TV, Stan Bonky, would-be MP decides to make a serious bid to get to Westminster.

How to go about it, and what to do? Many and various are the paths which lead to a seat in the Chamber, some are short and strewn with flowers, most are long, winding and rocky, and only successfully traversed by those who possess god-like powers, grim determination and endurance, and a skin somewhat thicker than that of a rhinoceros.

Although the approach differs widely depending on the political persuasion of the would-be MP, one thing holds true for Tory, Labour, Liberal, SNP, Ulster Unionist, you name it. The first law of getting elected is YOU CAN'T START TOO SOON.

Ideally you should join the party of your choice at the earliest possible moment. Remember, all this is leading up to the all-important selection meeting, and you can bet your granny's gravestone that your very first question will be from some old-timer at the back, who will ask you how long you've been a member of the party. The Labour Party is especially touchy about this, and if you can't give a reply in double figures you're likely to be in trouble as a nakedly ambitious parvenu, who's not been in the party ten minutes before putting themselves up for the top job. Even worse, if you stand there at the age of forty five and have to admit to a piddling six-year membership, the next question will undoubtedly be 'and why did it take you so long to join?' To which there is really no good answer. Labour is a deeply emotional party, committed to loyalty and the cause. It simply won't wash trying to explain to a selection meeting that you only joined aged thirty nine because before then you'd never really thought about it. The Conservatives are rather less hung up on such things, naked ambition being a positive virtue in their eyes. Michael Mates MP, when standing for selection in Hampshire East, was asked about his record in the Conservative Party. He firmly replied that if he was selected for the seat, he would definitely join. Nonetheless the Tories know the value of consistency, and are likely to be impressed by a solid track record.

Both major parties allow people of fifteen and over to join. Although most normal people would find it hard to suppress a shudder at the idea of some acned teenager spending every free evening discussing the implications of EC food subsidies when their better adjusted contemporaries are sniffing glue down the local youth club, party members see things differently. Anyone who joins their local party as a callow youth, providing they have the ability to string a reasonably coherent sentence together, and the courage to stand up and repeat said sentence at a public meeting, will be immediately marked out for great things.

All political parties like young people – they are, after all, the future – and will welcome any new recruit with open arms. As a youngster you can call on the help and support of the local party officers and top brass. Your ignorance will be forgiven, and your eagerness to learn will be commended. Labour Party stalwarts who would be moving expulsion orders against an adult recruit who mispronounced NACODS (knack-ods, never neigh-cods) or mixed up his T&G with his GMB, will smile tolerantly at the confused teenager and take time to explain. Likewise Tory grandees will gently point out to fresh faced innocence that the Monday Club are not a band from Manchester.

However, it is important to remember that youthful involvement, like so much in politics, is a double-edged sword. In the same ways as many of us shudder to remember the boy or girl we thought we were in love with when still wearing school uniform, so our political infatuations can be similarly short-lived. You should always bear in mind that a political party, like a puppy, is not just for Christmas but for life. You may have been in the SNP for three years before you realised that the Labour Party was right all along, but by then it's too late. If you swap allegiance you will spend the rest of your political career trying to live it down. There is always the exception that proves the rule. Winston Churchill, in the famous phrase, 'ratted and re-ratted', leaving the Tories for the Liberals, and then returning back to the Tory fold. David Owen managed to balkanise two parties, Labour and the Social Democrats, in the course of his parliamentary career, and survived. But for every Churchill or Dr Death, there's a thousand others, confined forever to political obscurity as a result of filling in the wrong membership card in their formative years.

The other thing to be wary of is getting carried away in the first flush of youthful exuberance. The Federation of Conservative Students and the Labour Party Young Socialists have both advanced some fairly out-to-lunch policies in their time and, on more than the odd occasion, loudly denounced their respective party leaderships for being traitors to the cause. When you're young there are few things more satisfying than thoroughly upsettinging the dreary old guard with the extremity and violence of your views, and watching them go into shock as you put forward your plan to change the world tomorrow morning. However, all this can turn to dust when, your enemies having done their homework, some bright spark at the selection meeting asks you if you still support the IRA as you publicly avowed in 1987, or if you stand by your assertion, quoted in the local newspaper three years ago, that heroin should be legalised. In the world of politics things may be forgiven, but never forgotten, and a would-be MP who leaves behind him enough hostages to fortune to content Hezbollah, will have many years in which to repent at leisure.

Basically it is best to regard your early political years as a sort of apprenticeship. Like any apprentice you will be expected to take direction from your elders and betters as you learn the ropes. A wise would-be MP will watch and listen, garnering everything possible from the mistakes of others. He will cheerfully take on all sorts of dismal jobs that no one else wants to do – leafleting, addressing envelopes, running revolutionary jumble sales – knowing that one day this will be beneficially recorded as 'grass-roots commitment'. Most importantly, friends will be made, lots of them, who will one day turn out to vote, because after all, what all this is leading up to is that magic moment when the ballot is announced, the committee decide, and the safe seat is in the bag.

There are short cuts to Westminster. It is not unknown for a constituency to pass from one family member to another. But in the main there's no avoiding the arduous and long-winded process of being selected for a safe seat. To complete this Herculean feat successfully takes a great deal of time and effort, but what you do and how you do it depends entirely on which political party you have chosen as your vehicle to fame and fortune.

How to Be a Conservative Candidate

The Tories pride themselves on being the party of business, and why not, since they've actually bankrupted enough of them? They like to get on with things in a businesslike fashion. Slackers and shirkers are not welcome. With this in mind, the first thing to do is to get on the official Conservative Candidates' List. This may sound easy if you say it quickly; in reality it is a tortuous process best-suited to people one would-be candidate described as 'arrogant young rottweilers'. So, having wasted the golden years of youth being polite to vicious old ladies in hats at the local Conservative Association, spent untold hours delivering leaflets with John Major's picture on the front, and danced with every important person in sight at the annual fund-raising do, what is the next move?

First of all you have to write to Conservative Central Office – the party's headquarters in London's Smith Square – for an application form for the Candidates' List. The form when it arrives will be depressingly detailed and worryingly personal. It is designed to show up anything in your past life which may prove to be an embarrassment to the party. Informed opinion on this point strongly advocates lying through your teeth, because if everyone filled in the application form honestly, the Conservatives would very soon be left with no candidates from which to choose.

Once the form's been completed and posted back to Central Office, you sit and wait until you are summoned to an interview with the area agent. This is more or less a formality, mainly designed to weed out the total nutters. As long as you don't dribble, or claim to hear voices, you should be okay. If the area agent decides you are not wholly insane, you will then go on to a much grander interview with the Vice-Chairman of the party. This is where making a good impression starts to become important. The Vice-Chairman is the final arbiter when it comes to deciding whether your name goes on to the Candidates' List. It is never too early to start sucking up to him. At the interview you will try to show that you have sufficient political experience to make MP material. Here's where all those hours of drudgery come in very handy, and the years you've spent licking envelopes and bottoms single you out as a potential representative of the British people. You will also be questioned on your experience in what passes for the real world. Basically this means your job. At this point the best thing you can possibly say is that you were called to the Bar five years ago, or became a partner last year, and that your firm specialises in company law. If by some mischance you can't say this, you will have to try to make the best of a bad job. There is no rule to say a Yorkshire miner or someone who works on Gay Switchboard can't become a Tory MP, but very few do, and probably very few want to. The far-sighted prospective candidate will have taken this into account and studied law, preferably at Oxbridge.

You will be expected to turn up for the interview with the Vice-Chairman armed with plenty to say on your specialist political interests, as nominated on your application form.

There are two important rules here. Firstly ensure your interest is narrow, arcane and entirely peripheral to everyday political business. This has the advantage of allowing you to know a great deal about the subject (because the one book on the topic, published in 1979, contains everything anybody's ever said on the matter). It should also put you in the happy position of knowing more than the Vice-Chairman, who has better things to do with his time than mugging up the detail of the Cardiff Bay Barrage Bill. Conversely, it is a foolhardy would-be candidate who announces a passionate interest in the economy. You are more than likely to end up exposed as someone who once read *The Beginner's Guide to Monetarism* and only remembered half of it. The second thing to bear in mind is to choose an interest on which there is a clear party line, with which, of course, you agree wholeheartedly. Subjects such as Europe and capital punishment should be assiduously avoided. Your opinions are bound to irritate the tits off at least 50% of the people you meet, one of whom may be the Vice-Chairman. Stick to something like the vital importance of Britain's nuclear deterrent – anyone who disagrees with you will undoubtedly be in another party.

Having, with luck and judgement, overcome the hurdles placed in front of you so far, you are now faced with the final rite of passage. If you pass the Vice-Chairman's interview, you are then eligible to go the Candidates' Selection Weekend, a ritual of pain and humiliation beyond even Frank Bough's wildest dreams.

The weekend was one of Mrs Thatcher's innovations, and it is modelled on the Civil Service Accelerated Promotion Weekend. You arrive on Friday and leave on Sunday. Every moment in between you will be subject to intense and critical scrutiny.

As Cynthia Payne can testify, ritual humiliation doesn't come cheap. You will have to find £100 to pay for the privilege of turning up at all. On top of this there's the outfits. Men will need two suits (one for Friday, one for Saturday), black tie for the dinner on Saturday night, and something 'smart but casual' for Sunday. It is as well to remember that 'smart but casual' means a tweed jacket, Pringle sweater and open necked shirt – this is most definitely not an invitation to show just what a snappy dresser you can be in your leisure moments. Women are faced with a hideous dilemma. Are Thatcher suits in or out? Should Saturday night's dress be bold and assertive or calmly understated? Is it done to wear black? Is it best to be sexy and provocative, or elegant and discreet? Nervous candidates should comfort themselves by taking a quick glance at the Conservative MPs who made it. Standards are clearly not that rigorous.

The weekend will consist of many different segments. There will be interviews with industrialists and MPs, group discussions, role playing and mock debate. At the dinner you will be questioned by the person seated next to you, and at one particularly horrendous moment the Vice-Chairman will bellow down the table to ask your opinion on the common agricultural policy or Scottish devolution. You will also have to prepare an essay before you go, which will be written over the weekend. It is strictly against the rules to take notes or briefings of any kind. Everything you do will have to come out of your own head. It goes without saying that the temptation to cheat is overwhelming.

The horrors of the Candidates' Selection Weekend have been known to reduce grown men to tears. The prospective candidate should remember it is a situation which favours the aggressive. You are supposed to show qualities of leadership and initiative. This roughly translates as an ability to bully those weaker than yourself. Seize any opportunity to make other candidates look foolish. Don't be afraid to interrupt or drown out your colleagues' contributions. When all else fails, shout.

If you come through this baptism of fire you will be on the candidates' list, and thus eligible to apply for a seat. When a Conservative seat becomes vacant, the Chairman and Agent of the Association will set up a Selection Committee. The first thing you will do is send in your application. For a safe seat, there may be up to four hundred applications, and from these the committee will select about twenty to interview. It is not easy to secure interviews. An almost infallible trick is to ensure that you are local – however, for the Conservative seeking a safe seat living in say, Sheffield, this method obviously has its drawbacks. The best advice in these circumstances is to move to Surrey.

Once you have made it to the interview you will have to give a short speech, after which you will be questioned by the committee members, the majority of whom will be blue-rinsed old ladies in hats. The successful candidate will be the sort of person whom the old ladies would like their daughters to marry. This incidentally explains why there are so few women Conservative MPs. The male candidate, prior to this final interview, should pay close attention to hair (newly washed and shiny, a tiny bit on the floppy side), smile (open, engaging, boyish) and charming repartee. You should be relaxed and witty, a tad roguish, if possible – a hint of the lounge lizard. However, if Jim Davidson is your idea of a lovable rogue don't even bother trying. Cecil Parkinson, however, would seem to fit the bill nicely. Women should exude confidence, and remind the men on the committee of matron and their schoolboy fantasies, whilst at the same time calling up a faint memory of Mrs Thatcher. It is, surprisingly easy to do both at the same time. It is also vital to have a spouse, preferably your own, or at the very least a fiancée, whom the committee will also want to interview. People quite often succeed or fail at this stage on the strength of their partner's appeal. Hence the prospective candidate will have made the necessary arrangements before the selection interview, and with someone who can muster the right combination of dedication to the cause, dog-like devotion to the candidate, and a willingness to be asked impertinent questions by heavy-breathing colonels and be-permed battleaxes. There is a story of a would-be MP who missed out on a safe seat in the Tory shires because his wife turned up at the selection meeting wearing a stretch cat-suit in a leopardskin print with a silver belt. It is worth taking time to buy your wife or husband's selection outfit for them. Wives should be kitted out at Laura

Ashley, in soft prints and frills. High necks and long skirts are *de rigueur* and flat shoes are important. Husbands should wear a dark grey suit with a blue tie – both should speak only when spoken to.

Politically, Selection Committees tend towards the atavistic approach. Most Conservative Associations are obsessed by sex and violence. They will almost certainly be in favour of stringing up murderers, rapists and social workers. They will want to bring back caning and introduce corporal punishment into the prisons. They will also bang on about the horrors of homosexuality, abortion, sex education and single mothers. You must be prepared to endorse all of this wholeheartedly. Once in the House of Commons you can continue to oppose the death penalty or support a 'woman's right to choose' to your heart's content. The trick is to get there in the first place. Whatever happens, don't be down-hearted. Some of the brightest stars in the current Tory firmament have only achieved their pre-eminence at the cost of trailing round hundreds of Selection Committees before getting lucky. Also, be warned, you are most unlikely to be given a safe seat at first go. You will almost certainly have to prove yourself by standing in Sunderland South or Rotherham Central, and suffering three weeks of physical assault and abuse before waiting at the Town Hall and watching the Labour vote weighed in. If at the end of this you are thought to have given a good account of yourself, and, better still, upped the Conservative vote from 5 to 5½%, you will be set fair for better things.

How to Be a Labour Candidate

NB: All advice to Labour candidates should be checked against the almost weekly changes in selection procedures.

There are two paths to a safe Labour seat. Either you have to have the manipulative powers of Machiavelli (and similar scruples), or you have to have the immense good fortune to be in the right place at the right time to become the heir apparent to a retiring MP. There is a third road, although this is becoming increasingly unfashionable. The third way consists of being such a hopeless donkey and pain in the arse, that your political colleagues in whichever stronghold in Scotland, Wales or the industrial north, send you to Westminster to keep you out of their way. During the '70s it is alleged that one famous union leader got rid of the dross from his union by ensuring they were selected for parliamentary seats, thus making certain they were not on the national executive of the union, where they could mess up the important decisions. A certain British Euro MP owes his career to colleagues' determination to keep him off a particular Council. However, the times they are a changin', and as life grows more and more difficult for trade unions and local authorities, so the idea of using the House of Commons as a political dumping ground for the intellectually challenged has become discredited. The prospective candidate, no matter how stupid or socially inept would do well to remember this.

So what then is the best path for the would-be candidate to take in the Labour Party? If you're lucky you will be marked out as the favourite son (there are very few favourite daughters, although it has been known to happen), and when your constituency MP retires, you will sail into the seat on a swelling tide of good fortune.

To do this you must fulfil one absolute criterion. You will have to be local. But by local they mean *local*. This can create difficulties for a hopeful candidate. It's no good looking through the candidates' list for the last General Election, and noting that two of the Newcastle MPs are in their early seventies, whilst the Member for Sunderland is practically dead already. If this were the Conservative Party, upping sticks from Wiltshire, moving to the North East and learning the words to *Blaydon Races* might conceivably ensure you a look in as the various elderly incumbents drop from their perch. However, the Labour Party isn't like that.

The Labour Party believes in 'communities'. To be a member of the local community you have to have been there for about twenty years. For many areas with safe Labour seats you need to have been born there. If it's Yorkshire or Scotland, your parents ought to have been born there too. It is no good whatsoever hoping to be thought of as a local just because you relocated two years earlier, as part of your multinational company's executive reshuffle, to manage the phased redundancies at the shipyard. For socialist aspirants with the misfortune to be born south of Sheffield, it's also as well to remember that there are few things that exceed the deeply held and oft-expressed contempt of your bona-fide northern socialist for the soft south. They wouldn't spit in your mouth if your teeth were on fire. You will be mocked and mistrusted. It is possible to earn acceptance, but by common agreement this usually takes three generations.

If your parents have been sufficiently far-sighted to allow you to claim kinship with the industrial working class, then your next move is to get on the local council. The number of councillors who become Labour MPs is quite staggering. During your time in the council chamber you will have to perform a difficult balancing act. You must do enough to mark yourself out as a leader of men – a Committee Chair at the very least, preferably Leader or Deputy Leader of the council – but you must also take care to retain the respect and affection of your fellow councillors. Many a councillor-candidate has narrowly missed selection due to the block vote of embittered council colleagues. It is a galling experience, having spent five years working your way up from the Allotments Committee to within a hair's breadth of glory, to see the glittering prize snatched from your grasp because of the grudge held by the seven members of the Transport Committee, who hate you like poison, because you said their proposed trip to look at the Brazilian bus system was a waste of public money.

As can be seen, becoming the constituency dauphin is a lot more difficult than it sounds, and anyway, largely self-selecting. Most would-be candidates would do better to arm themselves with a copy of *The Prince*, and having studied Machiavelli's text assiduously, enter the fray, armed with a number of daggers. These will be judiciously placed between the appropriate people's shoulder blades.

So, eyes firmly fixed on Westminster, teeth gritted and knives in hand, the first thing to do is to find out the lie of the land.

The Labour Party is administratively split into regions: Scottish, Northern & Yorkshire, North West, Central, West Midlands, South East, Wales, South West and Greater London. Some of these, from the point of view of the would-be candidate, are almost a complete waste of time. Following the 1992 Election both South East and South West regions could boast only a tiny handful of seats. Things are, however, looking up, and the very astute and optimistic prospective MP might calculate that there are a number of possible seats in the south of England that will be Labour gains, come the next General Election.

On the plus side, such seats are easier to get hold of, as the competition is much less fierce. On the minus side, even if you win, you will spend the next five years having sleepless nights about protecting a majority of one hundred and forty five votes, and dedicating every waking hour to trying to ingratiate yourself with your constituents. You will also become preternaturally sensitive to the follies of your own party. As your smug and comfortable colleagues, sitting on majorities of 15,000 plus, call for re-nationalisation without compensation, or side with Saddam Hussein, you will mentally visualise the steady disappearance of the one hundred and forty five.

All these factors should be borne in mind before you make your next move, along with one absolutely vital ingredient, namely where do your friends live? For if there is one thing you need to be selected as a Labour MP, it is political friends and allies.

Having thought about all this, and weighed up the often considerable travel costs involved, you should ring up the regional organiser, who will tell you the timetable for whichever seats are up for reselection.

Reselection procedures will usually begin about two years after an election. They take place if the sitting MP signals a wish to retire, or if the constituency party is so hacked off with its present MP that it votes to have a reselection contest anyway.

The next move, having got the time table and the appropriate phone numbers from the regional organiser, is to pick your constituency, and contact the secretaries of the party branches and affiliated organisations. The first hurdle is to get invited by these bodies to their nomination meetings. Officially you are supposed to send a letter and CV to the secretaries, which they circulate to their members, who will hopefully vote to invite you, along with three or four others, to their nomination meeting. However, if young Stan Bonky is serious about this seat, there is much more to be done. This is the first opportunity, although far from the last, to call upon political friends.

If your friends are worthy of the name, they will then stand up at their branch meeting and say that they have been particularly impressed by one of the CVs on offer (yours) and that they would like to propose that you are invited to the nomination meeting. If your friends are cunning as well as loyal, they will have briefed somebody to second this proposal, and have people in place to do the same at all the other nomination meetings planned. Hence it's important to have reasonably astute friends, preferably ones who mix in a large social circle.

The other thing you can do unofficially at this juncture is actually to turn up in the constituency. Several years ago, Labour Party officers in a northern town were startled when their evening's viewing of *Coronation Street* was interrupted by an engaging young man knocking on their doors, and explaining that he was thinking of going for the seat, happened to be in the area, and thought how nice it would be to meet the Chair/Secretary/Treasurer/Education Officer, and so on, of the party. This worked like a charm, and he was duly elected, and is now on his way to the top. It is of course only a good idea if you are sufficiently attractive to be better value than *Coronation Street*. If you're a surly git with the social graces of a polecat, it's probably better not to bother.

Some branches and organisations will nominate on the strength of CVs alone, but most will invite a few candidates to attend a nomination meeting. At the meeting each candidate will go in separately, speak for five or ten minutes, and then answer questions for roughly the same amount of time. It is vitally important that you do your homework, and that you appear fluent and confident. Each party branch, trade union and affiliate will be different.

Talk to your friends and find out what's what. It is an incontrovertible truth that every Labour Party constituency has at least one trendy-lefty ward. The members of this ward will wear hand-knitted sweaters, holiday in Tuscany, shop at Sainsbury's and have kids with silly names. They will be lecturers in further education, or work for the caring professions. To impress this ward you should talk about the need for positive action on equal opportunities, and heavily hint that you disagree with the reversal of the party's anti-nuclear policy. The importance of proper crèche facilities cannot be overstressed.

In most constituencies there will also be what could be loosely termed the hardline-right-wing-bastards' ward. You should give them a speech in which the words 'realism' and 'pragmatism' feature heavily. You should also mutter darkly about the young men with sharp suits and portable phones who have taken over Labour Party headquarters. If you're a man you should turn up in a grey M&S suit with a CIU (workingmen's club) tie. Incidentally, if there's a Co-op Party branch in the constituency, you should always remember that the Co-op Party is the place hardline-right-wing-bastards go to die. The Co-op meeting will be full of grim-faced octogenarians wearing Co-op nylon shirts. They should be treated with the utmost respect, until you get out of earshot.

Most of the other party affiliates are self-announcing. The Irish Society want to hear about Ireland, and why we should pull out. The Black and Asian Section want to hear about racism. Women's sections are usually interchangeable with trendy-lefty wards. Poale Zion (a sort of Jewish section) want to hear that Israel should be allowed to shoot all the Palestinians on the West Bank. Finally, if you're in a university town, you are likely to have a NOLS (National Organisation of Labour Students) branch.

NOLS should be handled with care. Most NOLS members are hard-nosed political hacks with an eye to the main chance. It is only necessary to look at the past history of the apparatchiks staffing Labour Party HQ at Walworth Road in South London, or working for the Shadow Cabinet in the House of Commons, to realise that NOLS membership is the grounding for the true Labour Party politico. However, the way to win the NOLS vote is quite simple. Because they operate in universities and colleges, NOLS members wage a ceaseless war against loony left wing groups, for whom such places provide fertile breeding grounds. Most NOLS people are obsessed with hatred of those they term 'trots' (short for Trotskyists). This can cover anyone from Militant, Socialist Action, Socialist Organiser, Workers' Power, Labour Briefing – the list is endless. The thing that really cheers up your average Labour Student, is seeing a member of one of these entryist (a good NOLS term) groups being expelled from the Labour Party. All you have to do is call for an investigation to be set up into the infiltration of the party by various groups of trotskyites, with a view to their eventual expulsion, and the NOLS contingent will follow you to hell and back.

Finally at this stage, there are the trade union affiliates. The rules here are quite simple. Trade unions are interested in trade unions. They want to hear you talk about trade unions, their own trade union, that is. Hence when you go to the RMT (railway workers) branch, you talk about freight, the need to oppose the road transport lobby, and the evils of driver-only operated trains. If you go to NUPE (now part of UNISON) you talk about low pay, the unanswerable case for an increase in the health service budget, and the need to break down differentials. You should also remember that some unions hate each other, and that almost everyone hates the electricians.

Anyway, assuming your mates have done the business, and

that you have done your homework, you should end the first stage of the game with at least four or five nominations. The General Committee of the constituency will now draw up a short list of the six or so candidates with the highest number of nominations. A word of advice here for Stan. Don't over-do the nominations. If you look too promising too early, supporters of all the other candidates will club together in a 'Stop Bonky' campaign, and you might find yourself effectively squeezed from two sides.

Shortlisted candidates will be invited to write a six hundred-word statement, which the General Committee will send to every party member in the constituency. At this stage Stan might well be thinking that there must be pleasanter ways of passing his time, and that it would probably be easier to organise a *coup d'état* in Belgium than to win a Labour seat. This is likely true on both counts, and from now on the going gets tougher. There is no place for faint hearts within the Labour Party.

The six hundred-word statement poses a problem. If possible it should be all things to all people. The left should be able to use it as evidence of how right-on you are, while the right should be able to canvass support on the basis that your statement shows you to be perfectly in tune with the party leadership. Forget about being clever – otherwise you will just sail effortlessly over the heads of most of the membership. Try to be emotive. Key phrases such as 'blatant injustice', 'grinding poverty' and 'this great movement of ours' are always useful. Talk about the health service, education and the running down of our industrial base. As with the Tories, there are issues to avoid like the plague – Europe, the economy (never, but never use the word 'devaluation'), Sunday trading, or any one of the miners' strikes other than 1926, and not at all if it's a seat in Nottinghamshire. All of these topics are guaranteed to upset at least 50% of the membership, no matter what you say.

Once the statement goes out, the candidates are forbidden from personal canvassing. Here, yet again, is where the friends come in handy. Astute friends will organise groups of party members to meet for a drink, at which you will just happen to be present. Your friends should also identify the movers and shakers in various sections of the local party, and lobby them hard on your behalf. In the period between the statements going out and the final selection meeting or postal ballot, your friends should be working their nuts off.

If the constituency decides to go for a selection meeting, you will have to make a speech, probably about ten minutes long, and then answer questions for a further twenty minutes. This can be crucifying. By this stage most of the votes are already decided, except for a few floaters at the margins, but they may have the power to sway the whole thing either way.

Here is the final task for the local friends. They should be well positioned in the audience, armed and pre-briefed with a number of questions designed to show you in your best light. They will also have a number of embarrassing and difficult questions, which they will endeavour to put to your most dangerous opponent. What you must realise is that every candidate with any nous at all will be doing the same thing. If the party Chair is on your side, it's easy, as your friends will definitely be selected to speak. If not, be prepared.

If you have ever done or said anything foolish, the opposition will have found out, and you will be asked about it. You should expect the worst, and practise your response beforehand. For example, supposing you once made a speech supporting Militant, and some evil-minded party member asks if you really called Neil Kinnock a 'snivelling supporter of the capitalist hierarchy'? Don't, whatever you do, panic or shout. Smile. In fact, smile indulgently. 'We on the left have all had our problems with the pro-Tory media,' you say, 'and who can forget the appalling treatment Neil underwent at the hands of the tabloid press? Appalling, unjustified and totally unfair. But I'm glad you've raised the issue of party unity, because I have always thought that . . .'

By the time you finish they will have totally forgotten what the question was about in the first place. Which is another tip: long answers mean fewer questions.

The important thing to remember is that when the order of speaking is drawn, for reasons that will become clear, it is advantageous to go last.

Labour selection meetings are long-winded affairs, up to six candidates taking about half an hour apiece to speak and answer questions, plus the inevitable breaks for drinks and cigarettes, and then the voting at the end. To ensure the candidates don't get involved in an illegal last-minute arm-twisting, the clutch of would-be MPs are corralled into a room, set aside for the purpose, and guarded by a party member who ferries in tea and sandwiches.

This set-up, akin to spending a few hours on death row, will test the nerve and mental control of the would-be candidate to the limit. As you sit in the room trying to memorise your speech and consider your answer to possible questions on nuclear proliferation and the assisted areas scheme, you will watch your fellow contenders walk out to face the awaiting doom. Ears straining to catch the volume of applause following their speech, you will await their return. As the next candidate squares shoulders and marches for the door, everyone will cluster round the survivor, desperate for information.

What follows will be a game of masterly strategy. The returning candidate will want to say as little as possible; you want to drag out every last scrap of information. On your side are the rules of common politeness; all the returning candidate wants to do is call for a large brandy, and give you enough information to make you shit yourself, without telling you blatant lies. However, don't be put off. With skilful probing and persistence, you should be able to extract the briefing necessary to avoid walking in and falling flat on your face. What you want to know is simple. What is the mood of the comrades? How did it go down? And what sort of questions were asked? This last inquiry is vital. There are many Labour Party members who can safely be described as obsessive maniacs. Their whole lives are dedicated to a single issue. They can be relied on to have one question (which they will put to every candidate) designed to find out whether you know and care about the cause that consumes them. If you don't they will never forgive you, much less vote for you. It is vital to find out what the cause is, and how canny the questioner is likely to be.

Some obsessives are too single-minded to think about tactics and finesse. Their question will be something along the lines of 'Will you utterly condemn the contemptuous and barbaric practice of so-called doctors' use of innocent animals as the subjects of their disgusting, cruel and utterly disgraceful so-called experiments?' The would-be candidate who can't answer this one is a sorry figure indeed. Raising your voice and looking the questioner straight in the eye, you will reply, in ringing tones, that 'as a long standing member of the British Union Against Vivisection, I have no hesitation in utterly . . .'

However, not all the monomaniacs are so lacking in guile. Many are possessed of a deranged cunning, and this is where pumping those candidates unfortunate enough to come early in the draw is very handy. For instance, you may be well into your stride, dealing smoothly with the planted questions of your friends, when a scholarly-looking man with a pipe stands up to put the next question: 'Much has been said and written about possible changes in the age of retirement for men and women,' he declares, enunciating clearly, 'perhaps you could give us your personal view?' This is the political equivalent of the elephant trap. There you are, trotting happily through the forest when suddenly you become aware that beneath your feet the sandy path has disappeared, and instead you are staring into a huge pit, with sharpened stakes at the bottom. 'What on earth does the bastard want me to say?' you think wildly, so shaken that you can't even remember the current retirement age, let alone what has been 'said and written about possible changes'.

Of course it is impossible to cover every eventuality and before the meeting you should learn two or three phrases off pat, which should only be used in case of emergency. If some git of a party member bowls you a real googly, which leaves you completely clueless, invoke the crisis phrases, which roughly consist of – 'I think the real issue about the whole question of prisons/public transport/third world debt is' and then you go on to talk about something you do know about. So in response to the retirement age question, the taken-by-surprise candidate would reply: 'Yes, I think the real issue about the whole question of retirement is that pensions are no longer index linked, and . . . ' The 'very important point' strategy works in exactly the same way, as in 'You have raised a very important point about retirement, and much of the work I have done on the index linking of pensions shows . . .' Not only do these phrases allow you to twist the body of the question, but they give you a vital five seconds or so to think what you're actually going to say. Whenever such phrases are invoked, the prospective candidate must remember the tag line. After you've maundered on about index linking or whatever for five minutes or so, you pause, smile brightly at the questioner and say, 'and I hope that's answered your question?' It hasn't, of course, but fortunately he will not get an opportunity to come back and say so.

At the end of this longest day the vote will be held, and if you, and most importantly, your friends, have done their work well, you will be called to the front of the meeting to receive your accolade. For the unsuccessful candidates, this is pure torture. For the triumphant one it is a transport of sheer delight. Savour the moment. You, Stan Bonky, are on your way to Westminster. Because this is Safe Seat, and barring the unlikely event of your being assassinated by one of your vanquished opponents, you are practically an MP already, with only the ritual of the actual election to go through.

By-elections

Being a by-election candidate is like being a cork on the ocean, driven by the winds and tides, and with no control over anything, probably including your bodily functions.

If Stan Bonky considers standing in a by-election there are three things to bear in mind. Firstly, you must be beloved by the party hierarchy. This is a huge help in getting selected in the first place, and in the second place it means the entire weight of the party machine will be thrown behind you once you enter the fray.

Secondly, you must possess the sort of purity usually associated with the heroines of Victorian novels. If you ever smoked dope at university, slept with more than one person at the same time or dropped your trousers in the local pub, be sure the press will find out. If there are any secrets in your life you wouldn't wish to share with 50 million strangers, or any photographs in friends' possession you wouldn't wish to see on the front of the *News Of The World*, then by-elections are not for you.

Thirdly, you should have a willingness to obey orders usually associated with daleks. Any by-election, but especially important ones which hold out the possibility of historic victories or defeats, will attract the whole circus of professional politicos from party headquarters. There will be strategy people, policy people, press people, broadcast people, diary people, you name it. They will all have one thing in common; they will be your superiors, and they will ceaselessly tell you what to do. Any hint of rebellion on your part will go down like a cup of cold sick. You won't get away with it either. All that will happen is that the apparatchiks will send off a damning report of your conduct back to Walworth Road, or Smith Square or wherever, and then use their superior muscle to slap you ruthlessly back into line.

At the end of the day, if you have led a completely blameless life, and you are certain that none of your relatives are going to turn out to be up to their necks in the white slave trade, you may decide to go ahead and stand. If you do you should cheerfully wave good-bye to privacy and autonomy for the next three weeks.

Being a by-election candidate is rather like being a starlet in the heyday of the Hollywood studio system. The spotlight is on you. Every detail of your life and every word that you say is open to scrutiny, but you are essentially powerless. Behind the scenes are the men and women who are manipulating the whole show. They will tell you what to say and how to say it. What to wear and where to go.

To be treated like a defective child is irksome to most human beings, but during a by-election there's no help for it. The hopes and prestige of your party rest with you, and you are really nothing more than a small cog (albeit a cog of some significance) in the national party machine. So accept your fate. You may think that these smart-suited johnnies up from London know nothing about the real problems of Scunthorpe or Ayr or Mole Valley, but you'd be wrong. Although they may well have never set foot in the place (and you've lived there for fifteen years), they will probably know more than you do.

All the big political parties have very sophisticated by-election machines. By the time the sharp suits arrive in your patch they will know the local unemployment, small business, home ownership figures like the back of their hands. They will have a detailed record of the doings of the local council. They will know the percentage of the youth vote, the Asian vote, the pensioners' vote and any other vote you care to mention. Most importantly, they will be expert in dealing with the national media.

Until they arrive in Westminster, and in some cases long after, most candidates' experience of the press is confined to the odd press release or letter sent in to the *Bolton Chronicle* or the *Wythenshawe Recorder*. Most editors of local newspapers are so desperate for stories they will print anything, and will be grateful that you've filled a space. Facing Fleet Street's finest at the by-election's daily press conference, the would-be candidate will need all the help that's going.

Suddenly, instead of amiable old Fletcher, the editor of the *Chronicle*, who always comes for a drink down the Crown on

Friday night, you will be faced with a snarling pack of hell hounds, whose main aim in life is to catch you doing or saying something you wish you'd never even thought of.

If you are overweight, as was the case with one Labour by-election candidate, they will make you look grotesque by photographing you from the most unflattering angle. Worse still, they will probably dig up some sort of expert to construct a diet for the obese, which they will then print next to your picture. In the Bradford North by-election of November 1990, the Tory candidate, Joy Atkin, sent out election material containing a photograph of her posing in a graveyard. Happy journalists had a field day with endless jokes about the Conservative vision of Britain's future. Peter Tatchell, who went through untold horrors in the Bermondsey by-election in February '83, recalls journalists regularly rummaging through his dustbins in the hope of finding something of interest. Part of his problem was that due to a political disagreement, the Labour Party machine never really supported him. Because of the muggings handed out by Fleet Street and Wapping to a series of Labour candidates, the National Executive Committee of the party changed the rules to allow by-election candidates to be imposed. The Tories, following a few of their own disasters, have expressed envy of this system, and will doubtless introduce something similar.

At the end of the day, Stan Bonky would do well to think long and hard before standing for a by-election. Win or lose, you will go through three or four weeks of indescribable hell, after which your family and friends will have probably left you, and your self respect will have gone with them. If you stand for a safe seat, you risk an upset – that, after all, is what by-elections are about. If you stand in a marginal or no-hoper and secure a famous victory, you will undoubtedly be fêted for fifteen minutes. However, come the next General Election, you will almost certainly lose the seat, as the voters, away from the by-election sound and fury, revert to type and ancestral voting patterns.

The far-sighted would-be candidate will avoid all this. Compared to the heavy slog of the party selection procedures, the by-election may seem to offer a seductively quick and glamorous route to Westminster. Unfortunately, like the songs of the sirens, the dream of by-election glory more often ends with shipwreck and disaster. The wise candidate will know that there is no substitute for the safe seat with a solid majority. After all, the last thing a new boy or girl at Westminster needs is nagging worries about losing the seat so recently and so painfully gained.

Chapter Two

How to Be a New Boy or Girl

That Election Campaign

There are hearty and enthusiastic MPs who will tell you that they love campaigning. These people are either lying or mentally deranged. Campaigning is hell on wheels. Four weeks of ceaseless hard work and hysteria which brings out the worst in everyone. Tempers fray, arrangements go completely awry, cock-ups occur on all fronts, and everyone blames everyone else, but most of all, they blame you. As the candidate you are the focus of the campaign, and although the party workers are theoretically flogging their bollocks off for a Labour victory, or a Tory or Liberal victory or whatever, deep down, as they trudge the streets in the pissing rain, their resentful souls will whisper to them that all this effort is purely for the glorification of Stan Bonky, whom they never thought that much of anyway. Your job is to prevent uncontrolled mutiny breaking out, avoid saying anything terminally stupid to the press, and be seen to work harder and longer than anyone else.

The other thing about election campaigns is that they are never more than a hair's breadth from violence and disaster. An SDP candidate called Bill Pitt was thrown off a balcony whilst canvassing (it was the 5th floor). Miraculously he survived, dusted himself down and went back into the fray – only to be bitten by a potential voter's rottweiler. Conservative Robin Squires, who is now a minister, knocked on the door of a constituent in Hornchurch, only to find himself confronted by a large and naked posterior, as the occupant of the house mooned at him – a dangerous position to adopt in the presence of a number of Conservative MPs we could name. In General

Elections, emotions run high, and stories abound of candidates' cars being vandalised, threats being uttered and missiles and punches being thrown. Christopher Chope, the former MP for Southampton, was beaten up whilst canvassing in the '92 General Election. In the same year an SNP candidate called MacRae, who had the misfortune to be a transsexual standing in Provan, possibly the toughest of the Glasgow seats – none of which could be described as a picnic – was issued with a long list of suggestions as to possible further surgery. The MP for Provan, known affectionately as Jimmy (I.R.) Wray, a former horse dealer and occasional second-hand jewellery seller, was pictured in the local press smiling cheerfully as he dissociated himself from the various threats.

In fairness, it has to be said that the Tories do have a tougher time of it. Labour candidates standing in no-hope seats (Surrey, Sussex, Hamps, Bucks, Berks) have to put up with nothing worse than total contempt, and the occasional loony in green wellies, holding a shotgun and shouting 'GET ORF MY LAND!'. However, picture the hapless Tory candidate sent up to grim industrial heartlands for the obligatory blooding in the unwinnable seat. Affable public school boys who've never been north of Knightsbridge are suddenly and cruelly catapulted into the heart of deepest Doncaster. When they get there it takes a day or two to acclimatise – the cold, the smells, the accents. But once they've found their sea legs, they bravely sally forth. What they don't realise (although they very soon learn) is that these places only see a Tory once every five years, and absence certainly doesn't make the heart grow fonder. In between times their inhabitants face the usual round of redundancy, unemployment, poverty and misery which has come to be expected under a Tory Government. Not surprisingly the blame is placed squarely on the '*bastaad* Government and the *bastaad* southerners', and Lo, let us Rejoice!, for one of the very same is strolling up the garden path wearing a big blue rosette. The words 'lambs' and 'slaughter' spring to mind. To adapt *Othello*, as they often do in Doncaster, Conservative folk lore is full of moving accidents by flood and field, of hair's-breadth escapes i' the imminent deadly breach, of being taken by the insolent foe. Being a Tory candidate in a Labour stronghold is, to use a technical term, a bucket of shit.

Whilst no one would seriously suggest abandoning election campaigns, they are surreal events. It simply is not normal to spend all day walking round wearing a rosette, confronting total strangers and trying to strike up a conversation. Although canvassing politicians are often accused of only being seen once every five years, imagine the annoyance of the punters if their MP, Jehovah's Witness style, knocked on the door on a weekly basis. The best advice is to try to be as normal as possible, even in near impossible circumstances.

Not surprisingly, some crack under the strain. A young man called Gallagher, who stood in Don Valley in South Yorkshire in 1987, placed a large advert in the local press prior to polling day. It bore the legend, GALLAGHER HAS DONE THE WORK! This was followed in slightly smaller type by *'including sausages and beans at Rossington Pit'*. What this might have been intended to mean is open to debate, but in terms of effective electioneering it could be called a *nul points* scenario. Perhaps the most hapless tale of all belongs to a Liberal called Mr Balls, yes, who commissioned election posters which advised the bewildered inhabitants of his constituency to VOTE BALLS! VOTE LIBERAL! In similar vein a Tory candidate called Keith Speed, now Sir Keith, and MP for Ashford, got in trouble with the local police when he peppered the by-roads of his rural constituency with posters which bore the instruction SPEED! Passing motorists had apparently taken him at his word.

Even after the day of victory, the humiliation heaped upon the politician by an uncaring general public does not abate. During the '92 election campaign, a prominent woman MP could be spotted somewhere on telly almost every day. After the dust settled and normal service resumed, an admirer wrote to her. 'I felt so sorry for you,' he said, 'being made to look ridiculous in those horrible clothes they made you wear. In future you should insist on being yourself.' Unfortunately 'those horrible clothes' had all been personally bought by the MP herself. Elections are truly a no win situation.

First Impressions

Well, you've finally made it. As the cruel light of morning pierces your raging hangover, you will suddenly leap out of bed and dance around in front of the wardrobe mirror, shouting YES! YES! YEE-EES!!! All thoughts of taking treble the recommended dose of Anadin and going to the bathroom to throw up will be forgotten. For it is the morning after the night of the General Election, and you, Stan Bonky, are now the MP for Birmingham Safe Seat.

Your elation is understandable. Christ knows you've worked for this moment. Years of sweat and planning. Hours of tedium, being polite to people you would happily see crucified upside down, not to mention the agonies of the campaign.

After a day or so, having recovered from the strains and excitements of the campaign, it will begin to sink in that you really are a Member of Parliament. What do you do now? Well it's up to you. There's no one there to advise you, no one to tell you what to do, or what to expect. You really are completely alone. The only official guidance you will get is a letter which will tell you when to turn up at Westminster to take the oath, which is an undertaking of loyalty to the Queen. This absurd anachronism is both completely cretinous and completely compulsory. If you don't take it, you can't take your seat. It doesn't matter whether sixty thousand people voted for you or not; no oath, no job.

Other than this rather meagre piece of guidance, the powers that be completely ignore the new MP. Much like the young wildebeest, you are supposed to be up and running of your own volition within hours of birth. If you're too feeble to keep up with the herd you are deemed to be a casualty of natural selection, and left to lie for the nearest jackal to pick off.

In recent years, there have been some attempts by the various political parties to institute induction courses for newcomers, which have mostly come about because of pressure from hacked off MPs, who after their election spend weeks wandering round the place trying to find out what they are supposed to be doing, and how they're supposed to do it. These courses have made some small improvement, but by and large, you are still basically left to fend for yourself. Dennis Skinner, for example, the day after his election as MP for Bolsover, simply turned up as usual at the pit to do a day's work. His former Coal Board bosses were extremely embarrassed and told him to go home. This may all sound a bit silly, but the point is no one tells you. Advice about the boring but necessary details of starting any new job is only just beginning to be offered.

When you do finally make your way to the Palace of Westminster, as a new MP you will become instantly aware of a meteoric rise in status. All doors are open to you and suddenly no one can do too much for you. Security guards and police who often treat members of the public as though they are all terrorists will now greet you in the role of faithful family retainer. 'Good Morning Sir!' they will cry, 'How are you Sir, and how is Mrs Bonky? No, don't bother to show your pass Sir, of course we recognise you.' They will recognise you because the locker rooms of security staff are adorned with pictures, not the usual locker room pictures ripped out from page three. No, the guards have been spending their off duty breaks memorising new MPs' faces from election literature photos. This is fortunate, because on day one you haven't got a pass. You know you're a Member, lots of people in Safe Seat know, but in London no one knows you from a hole in the wall. The key to all doors, and to instant respect, are the words 'I am Stan Bonky, the new MP for Safe Seat'. It is at this point that what have become very stringent security controls are at their most vulnerable, as security staff struggle to remember the inside doors of their lockers. For those concerned with such matters these are really underpant-filling times. Torn between the devil and the deep blue sea, the overstretched staff have to decide between the demands of security and running the risk of offending a brand-new MP who just happens to look like a member of the Baader-Meinhof Gang. This phase passes fairly quickly, as, assisted by the rogues' gallery in the locker room, security staff establish who's who.

Once inside, the new MP will find the House of Commons full of doors marked 'Members Only'. It's true that some of these doors lead into the men's toilets, but others open on to sumptuous libraries, rest rooms and bars. You will note some lifts marked 'Members Only' and others which staff have to vacate if Members want to use them. You will find out that as a Member you can (if you are sufficiently insensitive) jump the taxi queue in New Palace Yard, and steal the taxi of the humble assistant who has been waiting for the past ten minutes, shouting: 'Take me to the Carlton!' – MPs who do this receive numerous nominations for the Shit of the Year award. You will, in short, be treated like royalty. Stan Bonky needs to have a firm hold of himself, metaphorically speaking, because it is only too easy to get carried away by it all, and to start believing in your own enormous importance. If you do, you will end up being a total twat, and neither use nor ornament to the long-suffering people who elected you in the first place.

The most important privilege gained by the new MP is access to the Chamber. MPs are of course the only people who may enter, sit and speak in the Chamber once the House is in session. Almost every MP will tell you that when they first enter the Chamber as a bona fide Member, they feel an enormous sense of achievement, of having finally made it.

Being There

The problem with the House of Commons is that you don't know what the rules and conventions are until you break them. Peter Mandelson remembers striding towards the Chamber on his first day, only to be rugby tackled by an attendant, as he crossed the threshold. The reason for all this excitement was that Peter was carrying his briefcase, and it is strictly forbidden to carry bags into the Chamber. Few new

MPs know these arcane rules, and consequently they are end-
lessly put in the position of making wankers of themselves. A
number have never given up the habit.

Sebastian Coe suffered a hellish experience during his first
week. Teaming up with fellow new boy Gyles Brandreth (a
note of advice here, Seb, you can do much better than that),
the two MPs decided to have their first meal in the Members'
Dining Room, and at about 7.30 pm duly trotted down for
dinner. The place was absolutely packed, the only visible free
table being at the very far end of the room. Seb and Gyles
headed for it, and as they did so, they felt the eyes of the
assembled MPs following them. Not a naturally arrogant man,
but all the same an Olympic medallist and world-famous
athlete, Seb hints, but doesn't quite say, when telling this
story, that he assumed his fellow MPs had recognised him,
and were staring for that reason. Anyway, the distant table
reached, the two new MPs sat down and waited. Eventually,
and after quite a few more curious looks, the head waiter
approached at a stately pace, just about managing to keep the
smirk off his face. 'Good evening gentlemen,' he said. 'Seeing
as you are sharing his table, I assume you will be dining with
the Chief Whip and his party this evening?' The walk back
through the crowded tables seemed to last a lifetime, the stares
taking on an entirely new meaning.

But in fairness, how were they supposed to know? The answer
is, they weren't; like so much in the Commons, they were supposed to learn through bitter and humiliating experience. The
social niceties in the Palace of Westminster are sufficient to
give Miss Manners a nervous breakdown. The different
alliances, vendettas and groupings make a Renaissance court
seem a doddle, and the whole edifice is run on a complex and
rigid system of hierarchies and affiliations which should be
learned as quickly as possible.

After taking the oath and getting started, Stan will probably
begin to mill about with a crowd of fellow MPs who will consist of other newcomers, MPs from the same regional group,
and perhaps the odd mentor who is an old hand and an

acquaintance from pre-election days. The latter is most useful for showing you the ropes, explaining the more bizarre workings of the place, telling you where the bars are and generally looking after you and stopping you making more of an utter tit of yourself than is strictly necessary.

For example, as his mentor will explain to Stan, the House of Commons, not surprisingly, is obsessed with power and status. Those who have it guard it jealously, those who don't have its covet it, look up to it and fawn over it. Hence very real proprieties have to be observed when dealing with the top brass of whichever party. Stan will remember the second Tuesday of the election campaign when one of the party's big guns arrived in Safe Seat, went with Stan to canvass the sheltered housing complex and then appeared on Central TV, saying that Stan was an extraordinarily talented and fine man, and that he would be a shining star when the voters of Safe Seat obliged by sending him to the House of Commons. Stan will have treasured every word and moment. For said big gun it will have been no more than the third stop out of eight, in a wearying day doing the Midlands. He or she will remember that they did Stan a favour, just in case they ever need one in return, but otherwise they will have scrubbed every miserable moment spent in Safe Seat from their mind. It is therefore a very poor idea indeed for the newly elected Stan to go bowling up to the Home Secretary or Shadow Chancellor, and ask if he fancies a jar to reminisce about the happy time they shared in Sunnylands Retirement Flats. New MPs should speak to Great Men and Women only when spoken to, and they should cultivate at all times an air of grateful submission.

The other thing a mentor can do is to brief Stan on the horrors of the Chamber. It is axiomatic that no MP ever forgets the first speech or question. No matter what they have done before, no matter how eminent or public their previous existence, it is a moment of utter and paralysing terror.

The first time a new MP speaks, the maiden speech as it is quaintly called, certain rules and conventions apply. Actually in the House of Commons you can't buy a cup of tea without certain rules and conventions applying, but let that pass for the moment. By tradition, a maiden speech is heard in silence and without interruption, basically out of decency – to let the new Member find his feet and get acclimatised. The pay-off for this uncharacteristic restraint is that the speech should be non-controversial, and that its subject matter should generally be confined to the MP's constituency and to giving courtly thanks to the retiring or defeated Member. This can of course lead to some absurd essays in hypocrisy. Sometimes MPs fight for a seat against candidates from other parties they have a great deal of personal respect for. On other occasions the battle is bloody and bitter, and the stricken look of crumpled grief on your adversary's face is the thing that makes winning really worthwhile. If this is so, it is little short of ludicrous to have to stand up a couple of months later and spend twenty minutes telling the world what an exceptionally marvellous chap he was. If he was so bloody marvellous, you presumably wouldn't have stood against him in the first place. In more recent years, several MPs have decided to dispense with the time-honoured tradition and have left out the Cook's tour of the constituency (of absolutely no interest to anyone) and the insincere praise of their defeated rival (ditto) and actually tried to say something political. The pay-off is that the respectful silence rules also goes, and you can expect to be barracked.

Speaking in the Chamber is a big part of being an MP, and it is not an easy thing to do well, or indeed at all, partly because it is so gut-wrenchingly frightening. The horror of it all is hard to pin down. It's partly about the physical set-up of the place. When you get up to speak, you face the benches opposite which are full of your political opponents, whose expressions will be filled with disbelief, scorn and a complete lack of interest. It's partly about being on TV, but also there's the worry of standing up in front of people, most of whom are convinced they can make a better job of speaking than you can. You know that your fellow MPs will judge you harshly, and that you are speaking to an audience who are waiting for you to sit down and shut up, so that they can get up and start talking themselves. However, it is probably the cruelty of the place that makes it so terrifying. The Chamber of the House of

Commons is a Theatre of Cruelty. It knows no pity and no re-
morse. If you stumble or slip, the wolves will be on your heels
in an instant, dragging you down. Your own party colleagues
will not defend you. They will hate you for causing them
embarrassment, and their main desire will be to dissociate
themselves as completely as possible from your predicament.

Peter Mandelson was a national political figure before becoming MP for Hartlepool in 1992. Adept at handling the media,
confidant and strategist to the Labour Leadership, he was
probably about as far from a trembly kneed neophyte as it is
possible to get. His maiden speech, although nerve-wracking,
went okay. His next intervention in the Chamber was during
the debate on Maastricht. He had prepared very carefully,
thought out what he wanted to say, done the research, written
his speech out and half-learned it. When the time came he
stood up to deliver it.

For months later he looked haunted when recounting the tale.
His problems started, he says, when the Tories began their
interventions. Peter decided not to take any. He ploughed on
with his speech, and as he did so the clamour from the opposing benches grew ever louder as more and more Conservatives
tried to intervene. By this point he realised that he'd made a
mistake, but it was all too late. So thoroughly rattled by the
baying and howling around him, he clung to his text like a
drowning man to a straw. The further ten minutes or so it took
to finish seemed endless as the fury from the opposite benches
grew ever louder. On the Labour side he could feel the support literally melting away from him, as colleagues shuffled
down the benches to get away. By the time the torture was
over, the cold sweat was running down his back. Nothing in
life, he thought, can be more horrible than this.

There is little that Stan can do to avoid this experience. The
best and brightest of political debaters can regale you with
moments of utter humiliation. It does get easier with work and
practice, but not much. If you don't feel the tension and terror
in your stomach when you get up, the chances are you're over-
confident, and on your way to a major cock-up. There are,

though, obvious gaffes to avoid. Dame Elaine Kellet Bowman was trying to be nice to John Major during his travails on the Maastricht Bill in July '93. Outraged by Labour Leader John Smith's expert demolition job on the PM, she intervened during the speech. Wasn't it true, she insisted, that despite Labour's sneers, the French had a high opinion of the Prime Minister, and, to quote from *Le Monde*, were highly impressed by the way he was 'holding his own'? If this is true, it may explain a great deal about John Major's odd facial expressions, but in terms of helpful intervention, disaster is not too strong a word. A Tory MP, back in the Sixties, had a similarly unfortunate experience. When hearing that the new uniforms for the WRENS were to be put on indefinite hold until the gear for the Royal Navy had been sorted, the outraged MP got to her feet. Are the WRENS' skirts to be held up, she asked, until every sailor in the navy has been satisfied?

Prime Minister's Question Time is the twice-weekly big event which gives humble backbenchers their moment in the limelight and an unrivalled opportunity to get on prime time TV. All they have to do is stand up and ask the PM a question. It sounds easy, but it isn't. Witness the plethora of mangled questions, mispronunciations and lost punch lines, and that's only the Prime Minister. No matter how often you rehearse, you still have a fair chance of making a complete hash of it.

In 1989 a Tory backbencher got up to deliver his Question to the Prime Minister, and completely died on his feet. Forgetting the no doubt carefully rehearsed words, he was struck dumb by some malign force. Waves of jeers and verbal abuse crashed over him, whilst the same single thought went through the mind of every MP present, even those jeering the loudest – 'Thank God it isn't me.'

But witnessing such extreme horrors does not deter. It is the ambition of every Opposition backbench MP to get a Question to the PM that forces him to slump sobbing on to the despatch box and announce his resignation immediately afterwards. For Government backbenchers the object is to produce a Question which earns eternal gratitude and swift promotion. In both cases the dream remains elusive. The Prime Minister always possesses the last word, and even the most inadequate PM can usually dodge the elephant trap. The backbencher only has one Question, the PM has anything up to sixteen opportunities to indicate that he's not such a twat as his last answer suggested. Even getting the opportunity to put a Question is a problem. Twice a week a computerised shuffle takes place in the Table Office. Out of the four hundred or so MPs who hopefully submit their names, only ten will be in the frame. Not even the ten are guaranteed a chance. Much depends on the length of the PM's replies, the interruptions allowed, and the number of times the Leader of the Opposition chooses to intervene.

Another interesting dilemma which confronts the new Member is where to sit. It sounds simple, but like a lot of things in the House of Commons, it's anything but. Government and Opposition front benches are naturally taken up by Ministers and their Shadows. The new MP is faced with a bewildering choice of empty green benches, seemingly innocent enough, but in reality replete with more levels of meaning than the average semiologist would know what to do with.

Starting with the very furthest back bench. On the plus side you have the security of a 'back to the wall position'. Much like the stands at a football match, you can survey the scene and get a good overall view of the pitch and what's happening. There is also a bonus in telly terms, as when you stand up to speak you will be tastefully framed against oak panels, which are a distinct improvement on the baggy crotches of your colleagues which surround those seated lower down. Its drawback, is that it is a little distant from the main event.

There are also the spectators' or subs' benches. Way out on either wing, this is where you sit if you fancy a nap or have turned up to listen with absolutely no intention of speaking.

However, if Stan wants a career (and which MP doesn't?) the creeps' bench is the place for him. Directly behind the front bench, and pleasingly in camera shot, it's where PPSs sit to be close to the boss on the bench in front, and where all would-be front benchers sit, to cheer the speeches of their senior colleagues, snarl ferociously at the opposition and generally insinuate themselves with the leadership. It's also a very good position for offering to run useful errands.

As well as such seating blocks, there are also individual positions and smaller spaces which have been claimed by one group or another. Ted Heath always sits below the gangway, which has become a recognised place for ex-Prime Ministers.

On the opposite side, Dennis Skinner, Bob Clay, Dennis Canavan, Brian Sedgemore and others have founded a Labour hard left bench, which is just below the gangway from the Labour front bench, and directly in front of the Liberal Party. This is a fact which David Steel, David Owen, Roy Jenkins and latterly Paddy Ashdown have had some cause to regret, endeavouring to sound statesmanlike above the sneers and derision of Labour's awkward squad. It is also noticeable that following the '92 Election, Labour seems to be establishing a women's bench, which is coming into being behind the creeps' bench. There is, however, no such thing as an allocated place, other than for one day. To claim your daily place you must fill in a prayer card, and place it on a seat before prayers start at 2.30 pm. The parliamentary orisons are more usually attended by MPs enduring the experience in order to secure a seat, rather than being concerned about the future of their immortal souls. Sadly, most MPs are far more interested in a place in the Chamber than a place in heaven.

Kit and Kin

Clothes are important in a job where part of your effectiveness is tied into the impression you make. To be a properly dressed MP you don't have to look as though you've just spent £1,500 down at Jean Paul Gaultier or Chanel, but you do have to look smart, and above all clean. Over-ripe brie might be acceptable, but ripe MPs are not. The politician's clothes also have to be appropriate. This generally means suits for men and women. Stan Bonky may fancy himself as a bit of a rebel and sharp dresser, but if he arrives in the Chamber wearing a Gap T shirt and a leather jacket he will quickly realise his mistake. Likewise if he turns up in the same gear to draw the raffle at the annual Safe Seat Scout Jamboree, everyone under eighteen will laugh themselves silly, whilst everyone over fifty will tut-tut about declining standards in public life. Those in-between will spend the entire evening discussing his clothes rather than listening to what he has to say. The true rebel should remember the words of George Bernard Shaw: if you're going to say unorthodox things, then say them in orthodox clothes. Basically, people want MPs to look like, well, MPs. This means formal, and serious. You are, after all, there to represent them; they want to have some respect for you and this is difficult if you follow the example of one Labour MP and wear a crimplene safari suit and sandals with socks. Clothes have always been a problem in the House. Randolph Churchill caused a scandal by turning up in brown shoes – now there's daring for you – and Keir Hardie created an enormous stir by wearing a cloth cap. The dress code is immensely conventional; Michael Foot will never live down the 'duffle coat at the Cenotaph' story, but in fact his black coat was smart, expensive and respectable – it was just *different*.

Once kitted out in white Next shirt, double breasted dark suit from M&S and lively (that is *lively*, not something so blinding it causes accidents in the street) tie, Stan is ready to go mix it with the rest of the people's tribunes. Both Austin Mitchell, Labour MP for Grimsby, and Tory Minister Eric Forth could well benefit from toning down on the tie front. Oh, and whilst we're at it, the underwear. Some northern MPs will turn up wearing white terry towelling socks. These should be put in the bin as soon as they reach London. It doesn't matter that everyone wears them back home, they still look utterly ridiculous. Socks should be dark, cotton and fresh on each morning. Likewise the knickers scenario. Boxer shorts are best. Stan may be wedded to his comfy Y fronts, or if he's a bit of a goer, he might be labouring under the delusion that the black posing pouch he bought on holiday is just the thing. Well it isn't. Not only are such garments crushingly unsexy (in this context sexiness isn't important anyway) but the tight elastic leaves a line which shows through your trousers. It is of no use talking with weight and perception about the floating pound and the ERM if your audience is transfixed by your VPL. It also goes without saying that the John Major style of tucking the shirt in the underpants, so that you get a nice line of white cotton above the trouser belt, ought to be avoided.

The thing Stan has really to remember is personal hygiene. The Commons isn't known as Halitosis Hall for nothing. Bad breath, BO, sweaty feet and dandruff abound. Some MPs seem to find something deeply inimical about soap and water. When he chooses his London flat, Stan should make sure that it has a good shower, an efficient hot water system, and most importantly, a washing machine. The possession of this basic consumer durable will mean that Stan has no need to follow the example of one Scottish colleague, who parcels up his dirty smalls in a House of Commons envelope every week, and sends them back to Bonnie Scotland for his wife to wash. He will also avoid upsetting his staff, as in the case of another Scottish MP. The MP's researchers couldn't understand why the office smelled so horrible. In the end, after rooting around, they opened one of the drawers on the MP's personal desk. It was full of fetid socks and Y fronts, which had been mouldering away for months, and were almost at the stage where they could have walked to the launderette on their own.

Once he's got his gear, made his maiden speech and secured a place on the creeps' bench, Stan can start to think about making friends.

Friends in the House of Commons are almost always political. The protocol on social relations with members of opposing parties is in fact quite simple. There are no end of Tory, Labour and Liberal MPs who will have a cup of tea or a drink together. There are some who will share dinner, have a joke and generally enjoy each other's company. At the end of the day, though, they are acquaintances, not friends. There is an invisible boundary which cannot be crossed. You may have the same sense of humour, you may agree on certain issues (abortion, foxhunting, whatever), but deep inside you know that you only met because you both ended up in the House of Commons representing completely different world views. In terms of trust and common ground, shared assumptions and many of the other things that real friendship is built on, this makes the cross-party liaison a complete non-starter.

In the same way it is unusual for people on opposing wings of the same party to become friends. It sounds like political dogmatism, but it isn't really. It's just a matter of disagreeing about too many things too much of the time. Stan should be careful about choosing his friends. The more he has the better, but his 'special' friends are a different matter. If he becomes obviously and visibly close to one or two people, his fortunes will be influenced.

This can work well for him, but they have to be the right people. For example, Michael Mates, Keith Hampson and Michael Heseltine have ridden the ebbing and flowing tides of fortune together, whilst Gordon Brown and Tony Blair are the Roland and Oliver of the House of Commons, so intertwined they are virtually inseparable. There are other 'couples' in the House whose close friendships were either forged before becoming elected, or are based on very close shared interests or adjoining constituencies. But for the really ambitious MP, the thing to do is to latch on to a rising star, and rise with them. The idea that such MPs hang around with people because they actually like them can be dismissed as a piece of tragic naivety.

Staying There

What Stan should never, ever forget is that you can't be an MP without a constituency. The lure of London and the delights of swanning about in the Palace of Westminster may seem a great deal more exciting than dreary old Safe Seat. But if Stan falls into this way of thinking, he is really missing the point. Dreary old Safe Seat is the reason he went to Westminster in the first place. If he thinks the place is such a dump, then he really didn't ought to be representing it. There are a number of cautionary tales about MPs who have become too lofty for their constituencies, and subsequently paid the price. Robert Kilroy Silk, when MP for Knowsley North in Liverpool, apparently used to turn up in his constituency on an occasional basis, travelling up from London by Rolls Royce. The comrades in Militant were not at all amused by this behaviour and made his life an utter misery. Likewise Julian Amery, formerly the MP for Brighton Pavilion, spent most of his time, when not at Westminster, living in his house in France. His cheerful continental excursions were somewhat curtailed when the local paper's front page carried a full-size picture of him sporting the banner headline HAS ANYONE SEEN THIS MAN? Former Member Eldon Griffiths was often referred to as the MP for Orange County in California, since he seemed to have such a liking for the place, whilst Rupert Allason, MP for Torbay, has on occasion been called the MP for Bermuda North, as a result of his holiday home there and the jealousy of his colleagues.

However, minor scrapes and dalliances aside, MPs are on the whole pretty respectful of constituency opinion. This was not always the case. Witness Anthony Henley, MP for Southampton, 1727-34, who wrote to his constituents in the following terms, when they had dared to protest to him about the Excise Bill:

Gentlemen,
I received yours and am surprised by your insolence in troubling me about the Excise. You know what I very well know, that I bought you. And I know what perhaps you think I don't know, you are now selling yourselves to somebody else; and I know what you do not know, that I am buying another Borough. May God's curse light upon you all. May your houses be as open and common to all Excise officers as your wives and daughters were to me when I stood for your scoundrel Corporation.

Yours etc,
Anthony Henley.

It has to be said that they don't make 'em like this any more.

Constituencies are rather like lovers. They can be jealous, moody and difficult, demanding and embarrassing, but because you love them you put up with it. A great deal of the new MP's time should be devoted to consolidating the local position. This involves working with the local party or association to make sure that it remains active and to ensure that it isn't taken over by extremist loonies out to get rid of you. An active local party is the best insurance against falling majorities.

The other thing to do is to employ good and assiduous staff and to open an office and advice centre where people can come with their problems about housing, drains, the new one-way system, immigration, noisy neighbours and so on. In addition to this you should hold regular local surgeries and make sure you have a strong press profile on any important local issues. People like to see their MP doing something; it's not too much to ask, so you should do your best to satisfy this modest demand. 'A good constituency MP' is usually the phrase used about recently deceased MPs when no one can think of anything else to say, but if you actually are a 'good constituency MP', you will have the glowing satisfaction of knowing that you are doing the job for which you were elected – and on top of that making sure of getting elected again the next time round.

The Tribes of Westminster

When Stan first arrives at the House of Commons, he will find himself facing a whole new world, peopled by strange beings who practice outlandish customs and rites.

Everyone has heard that new MPs can't get office space, and frequently find themselves camping out in a corridor without desk or telephone. Unlike many modern myths, this is actually true. The new Member may well wait months before being allocated a desk, and when he or she finally gets one, it is almost certain to be in a room shared with at least one other MP. The Westminster powers that be have estimated that it will be the end of the century before every MP can be guaranteed an individual office. The new MP will also discover that by the time they have located the post office (this has been known to take about seven days – the first four wondering why no one's written to you, the next three trailing round trying to find where the letters are), the accumulated mail will fill several body-sized bags. Thus the unfortunate newcomer will immediately start with a huge backlog of work, and will spend the remainder of their political life running to stand still.

There are two ways of alleviating this misery. Firstly you can opt to follow the time-honoured principle of doing nothing at all. One new MP was shocked to see a long-serving Member collect his mail from the post office, take a cursory look through the envelopes to extract any cheques or personal mail, then happily dump the rest straight in the bin. The new Member remonstrated: 'you can't do that,' he said, 'what if the letters are important?' 'If they're important,' replied the old hand, 'they will write again', 'But how will you know if they have written again', said the new boy, 'if you never open the envelopes?' The old hand merely mentioned the size of his majority and said by the time they found out he would be collecting his pension. Another retiring Midlands MP informed his eager successor that he had managed to get the mail down to 'about seven letters a week' (bear in mind most MPs get at least fifty letters a day). How had he achieved this feat? By dint of never answering the letters – 'they soon get fed up of writing'.

Some mail barely deserves an answer. The keen new MP will eagerly file for future reference the glossy publications, annual reports and briefings which arrive on a daily basis, covering every topic you've ever heard of, and a few you wish you hadn't. After only six months into the parliamentary term the office will begin to resemble an outpost of the British Library, and the MP will realise that the majority of these corporate offerings should be thrown straight in the bin. There may be one MP out there who reads *Concrete Quarterly*, the periodical of the concrete industry, but if there is, they have yet to reveal themselves. Four times a year the bins of the House of Commons overflow with unwanted copies. A strong candidate for the most tasteless piece of junk mailing sent to MPs must be the cross-section of a womb, complete with developing foetus, commissioned by SPUC, the anti-abortion group. The House was debating the question of the upper limit on abortions at the time, and the mailing was intended as a lobbying device to influence MPs. It was, by common consent, entirely unproductive. One Tory MP allegedly wrote to SPUC to ask why they had forgotten to including the cooking instructions.

As far as the mail's concerned, the doing-absolutely-sod-all strategy can only be implemented if your majority is well into the rock solid twenty thousand band, and your local party or association is so moribund and uncritical as to be practically dead. A few such seats can still be found, but they are becoming rare. Faced with bags of bulging mail, Stan would be well advised to consider the second plan of attack. This consists of setting up a parliamentary office, getting some staff and doing some work.

All MPs are entitled to an office allowance. Currently standing at around £40,000, it is for paying staff wages, buying office equipment and paying constituency office bills. It sounds (and indeed is) a lot of money, but it is actually quite mean. If an MP is to operate properly, he needs the equipment and help to do so, and constituents have a right to expect a good and efficient service. To provide this an MP will need an office in the constituency as well as one at Westminster. Both offices need staff and equipment. Anyone doing sums in their heads will quickly come to the conclusion that the office allowance money doesn't adequately meet these needs – hence the number of student interns and voluntary helpers taken on by MPs. It's also a disincentive to work. Any MP who gets involved with emotive or controversial issues, such as animal rights or abortion, will be rewarded with a hugely increased workload. Similarly the MP who wants to run a specialist campaign, or get down to detailed political research. For example, pity the Shadow Cabinet Member, who with a research team of two or three, is supposed to effectively combat an entire ministry full of civil servants. As someone once said, you gets what yous pays for. It might also be a helpful innovation if this money were to be administrated centrally, as there is probably still the odd MP who gives the entire whack to his wife or lover, and then happily continues to put the letters in the bin.

If Stan does the decent thing, and starts to set up an office in the House of Commons, he will have his first brush with the Tribes of Westminster, because he will need a parliamentary secretary, and if he has any ambition, he will also want a political researcher.

Secretaries

unlike researchers, these fall into distinct party categories. Labour secretaries are often quite young, mostly women but quite a few men, have a tendency towards scruffiness and, in addition, a deep and abiding passion for politics. They would really much rather be researchers. Occasionally Labour MPs benefit from professional secretaries who are staggeringly good at their jobs, politically committed and slightly sharper than a bagful of razor blades.

Tory Seccies (to use their House of Common nickname) are a different breed. They are almost exclusively female and fall into two groups. The first group is aged eighteen to thirty five, and much given to wearing pie-crust collars, big skirts, velvet head-bands and stiletto heels. They will be called Annabel or Fiona, be single, from a good family, with a hungry look in their eyes, which will be focused on marriage, or at least a relationship, with a Tory MP. The second group will be thirty five to ninety. They wear bristly tweeds and will have been with their MP for twenty-odd years. Although often apolitical, they will nevertheless have a ferocious loyalty towards the boss, whose life they run with faultless efficiency.

Researchers

are basically a type, whichever party they work for. About
70% are male, with the more men the higher you get up the
political hierarchy (now there's a surprise). Above everything
they will be very clever. They will also be ambitious, and will
probably have a better political grasp than the MP who
employs them (with some MPs that's not so hard). Some are
specialists in their field, and will work in a specific policy area
(defence, Ireland, economics etc) whereas others are through
and through politicos, and will stick with their boss as he or
she changes front bench portfolio. Good researchers are worth
their weight in gold. They will write speeches, press releases,
articles and policy documents, and give advice on everything,
from how you look on TV to what your colleagues really think
of you. Because they have no need to compete with each other
professionally, researchers tend to know, like and chat to each
other (unlike MPs). They therefore have one of the most effective political networks in the House, cutting across inter-party
squabbles and jostlings for preferment. If their boss is considered a complete prat by his or her fellow MPs, the
researcher will know, because the other researchers will tell
them. They also have all the best gossip, and will know who is
sleeping with whom in technicolour detail. Worth £25K, at
least, of anybody's money. Which of course doesn't leave
much of the £40K to play with.

American Interns

American students, often studying politics, who come over as
part of a Stateside university course and can stay for as much
as a year, or as little as six weeks, though the usual stint is
about three months. Young, keen and often totally clueless as
to the intricacies of the British political scene ('just who is this
Paddy Ashdown guy?'), they are frequently shamelessly ex-
ploited by the MPs they're assigned to, ending up as
chauffeurs, photocopiers and tea makers. They also have
problems with language barriers. An MP's researcher was
shocked to be asked by her resident intern about the protocol

of 'wearing pants' in the office. 'I haven't worn them so far,' the girl said, 'because they told us not to, but I'd feel a lot happier if I could.'

The other Tribes are not office bound, but Stan would be well advised to know them, because they have it in their power either to smooth his path or to make his life miserable.

The Speaker

Is very, very important, and also a world-wide TV mega star. Being on the right side of the Speaker is vital, as it will affect your chances of being called to speak in the Chamber. Your approach to this august figure can be neatly summed up in two words – grovelling reverence.

Officers of the House

Basically civil servants, some of whom are very senior. They control the running of the place and staff the Table Office (where you go to put down Questions and EDMs) and the Vote Office (which stocks Bills, Acts, Hansards, White Papers and so on), and importantly, they service the Committees, both Standing and Select. In addition there is a large library staff. They are invariably skilled, helpful and friendly. They put up, in the main pretty cheerfully, with the most abstruse and ridiculous requests, all of which have a deadline of yesterday. There is a story of a group of Members, who being in the midst of a convivial time in one of the House of Commons' Bars, decided to sing the *Banana Boat Song*. The MPs then realised that none of them knew the words. Nothing daunted, they rang the library (it was after midnight) and put their request. Shortly afterwards the harassed librarian appeared in the bar with a photocopy of the required lyrics. Library staff really do serve above and beyond the call of duty. Stan should remember to be as nice as he possibly can and write thank-you notes after the miracle has been performed.

Security Staff

It is sad to observe that security arrangements at Westminster have got tougher by the year, and are constantly increasing. Photo passes are required for all MPs and staff, and are increasingly needed to facilitate movement around the House, which is becoming full of electronic doors and tardis-like people-sized glass tubes. There is a bewildering range of security personnel: police in uniform, police undercover, police dogs (for sniffing explosives). There are also private security staff under the control of the Serjeant-at-Arms. He is responsible for the overall safety of the Palace and, to inspire confidence, wears an 18th-century costume of black silk stockings, frock coat and sword. Also under the command of the Serjeant-at-Arms are the attendants, who deal with messages, the directing of the general public and some aspects of security. Men in their forties and fifties, they are reputed to be ex-marines, paras and SAS. They certainly look tough enough, despite having to wear the same eccentric uniform as the Serjeant (minus knee breeches, silver buckles and the sword). When not attending to duties they can be heard swapping tales of military exploits. Strange to report, the Serjeant-at-Arms and his Deputies are all ex-officers, most ex-Guards, whilst the attendants, or badge messengers, as they're called, are mostly ex-NCOs. Naturally they are all male and all white. Even Black Rod is disappointingly white. These are the people who stop visitors in the public gallery from nodding off, picking their nose or screaming abuse at Members at work on the floor. The whole operation is run with military *esprit de corps* and precision.

Catering and Cleaning Staff

These are the cooks, waiters and cleaners who keep the entire place up and running. Unlike anywhere else in the House of Commons, including the Chamber, here is a much more accurate reflection of the ethnic diversity of British society. In other words, there are lots of Black, Hispanic and Irish people employed. They often work very long hours, as some facilities have to be kept open as long as the House is sitting, which can easily be till two or three in the morning. Because the Commons wasn't built to cope with anything like the numbers it houses, they have to put up with all the difficulties of trying to feed and clean up after too many people in too small a space. The vast majority do their jobs well, and then sensibly get the hell out as soon as their shift finishes. The occasional character rises above humdrum everyday concerns, and becomes famous. Nora, who runs the House of Lords Bar, is an awesome figure and is rumoured to have a PhD in unsolicited and gratuitous rudeness. Richard, on the till in the restaurant of No. 1 Parliament Street, is the Chair of his local Tory Association in Dulwich, and argues amiably with Labour researchers, whilst Jean in the Members' Tea Room is rumoured to have a crush on Hugh Dykes, Tory MP for Harrow East. A suggestion so outlandish as to defy belief.

At the time of writing, and subject to correction, there is no Black person in any senior position within the House of Commons' hierarchy, amongst the thousands of people who work inside the Palace. The Black MP for Hackney North and Stoke Newington, Diane Abbott, made her first visit to the Members' Smoking Room shortly after being elected in 1983, where a number of Tory MPs mistook her for one of the cleaners. Clearly there is still a great deal to do to break down the institutional racism which would seem to exist within the Houses of Parliament.

New MPs will find all this out by trial and error. After a few months, Stan will have begun to get the feel of the place and will be starting to feel at home. The settling-in period is over. The next thing to do is to think about that career.

Chapter Three

How to Get to the Top
of the Greasy Pole

Politics, like other jobs, has its career structures, sackings and promotions, golf-playing executives and resentful tea-makers. The difference is that, unlike most professions, there is no clear and understood way to get on. Advancement comes through a mixture of luck, ability, cunning and assiduous brown nosing. The trick is to be in the right place, with the right people at the right time. Some MPs can wait years for their boat to come in. For others the path to fame and glory is swift, and they reach high office with the sort of effortless rapidity which earns the admiration of the press and general public, and the undying resentment of their colleagues.

Actually, whatever you do, there is no substitute for a large dollop of luck, but as the proverb says, 'God helps those who help themselves', and if you make the right moves, you can, to some extent, speed things along a bit. So many variables are at work that it is almost impossible to make a fool-proof master-plan for a quick shin up the greasy pole, but there are some advantages to be gained and blunders to avoid.

The Smaller Parties

The best advice to the really ambitious MP is don't bother to join in the first place. Becoming an Ulster Unionist is not the way to get to that Group Seven Summit of world leaders. There are many drawbacks to being an MP for the Liberals or one of the other smaller parties. The most obvious is that you have virtually no chance of ever getting into power. The best you can hope for is a hung parliament, which will mean that your handful of MPs get a chance to influence whichever of the larger parties makes up the Government. The last time this happened was the fairly inglorious occasion of the Lib-Lab pact in the 1970s: a grim experience for all concerned, leaving everyone involved with enough egg on their faces to make a very passable tortilla. Although it should be pointed out that in the 1992 Parliament it became clear that some kind of a deal was arranged between John Major and the Ulster Unionists, which allowed the Government to force through the Maastricht Bill, minus the social chapter. Time will reveal the full extent of the price, although everyone involved has hotly denied that any understanding exists. Indeed the Ulster Unionists declared that they 'asked for nothing and received nothing', leading one Labour MP to declare that at least they knew their worth.

British politics, with its current first past the post system, isn't very big on pacts and power sharing. The majority of MPs have enough of a struggle sharing power with people in their own party, never mind involving outsiders. This may change, but don't hold your breath. As things currently stand, Paddy Ashdown, the Leader of the Liberal Democrats, has probably about as much chance of being Prime Minister as Alex Salmond MP (leader of the Scots Nats) has of being the first President of an Independent Scotland.

However, for the likes of Liberals such as Matthew Taylor, MP for Truro, or Charles Kennedy, MP for Ross Cromarty and Skye, there are compensations. The struggle to the top of the party hierarchy has little or no meaning. There are only twenty two Liberal MPs, ranged against two hundred and seventy Labour and three hundred and thirty four Conservative, although by-elections will probably increase their number. When you recall that the Government has over eighty members including whips, but excluding dozens of PPSs, and that these ministers are shadowed by around the same number of people on the Labour front bench, you begin to appreciate the magnitude of the task which faces the Liberal Democrats and the other smaller parties. As a Liberal MP it's not so much *if* you get a position, more whether you'll be able to cope with the half a dozen jobs they will pile on to you. You could quite easily find yourself spokesperson for employment, small businesses and fishing, as did Scottish Liberal MP Jim Wallace before the 1992 Election. To cover this sort of ground properly demands the Renaissance man skills of a Leonardo or an Erasmus. On the plus side, you will, unlike your Tory and Labour opponents, get endless opportunities to reply to debates in the House of Commons, and lots of chances at telly.

Assuming that the smaller parties suffer from the same personnel problems as the two major players, half their MPs will be mad, bad and dangerous to know, and therefore not safe to let loose on TV without a nurse or standby. Hence if you are a Liberal Democrat, and reasonably bright and presentable, you will find yourself whizzing from the Six o'clock News to Channel 4 Seven o'clock, to News at Ten. Somewhere in between you will have stopped off for a quick radio interview to give your views on the importance of testicular cancer screenings or the like. By the end of all this you will be lucky if you can tell the difference between the NHS and the IMF. But you will do it, because you have no choice and there's no one else. Charles Kennedy, in his early thirties, is already the President of the Liberal Democrats. He speaks for the party on the European Community, and is a media veteran of such renowned political programmes as *The News Quiz, Have I Got News for You* and a host of others. Mr Kennedy is bright, capable, witty and carries his many responsibilities lightly. It is, however, fair to say that no matter how bright, capable and witty he might be, he is most unlikely to have gone so far so quickly in either of the major parties. The competition is simply too hot.

The two major parties are really a very different can of worms. For the hapless new MP looking around for how to make a mark, it can all seem a bit overwhelming. The way to get to the top will depend on which party you are in. Each has fairly precise requirements.

A Leg Up in the Labour Party

The overriding and essential element for doing well in the Labour Party is to make a great play of not wanting to. 'Careerist' is a term used freely in Labour Party circles. It is an utterly damning phrase, implying that you care nothing for the huddled masses yearning to break free, the wretched of the earth that you supposedly came to Westminster to represent. No, you don't give a toss about the unemployed, the pensioners, the miners and single parents. All you care about is your career. If this suspicion is allowed to get about, it will ensure that your putative career never leaves the runway. The Labour Party believes its MPs are elected to fight for the cause, the working class and a better world. If they find out they've sent someone to Parliament whose sole aim is to get their sticky hands on a ministerial red box and a chauffeur-driven car, they will not be happy. Even 'ambition' is a difficult word in the Labour Party. Greatness should be thrust upon the unwilling recipient, who will agree to accept unwanted honours strictly for the good of the party and the country.

Having committed this vital lesson to memory, the first sniff of preferment the hungry new MP will get is the offer of a committee place.

The House of Commons has two sorts of committees; Standing Committees, which deal with the Committee Stage of a particular piece of legislation, and Select Committees, which meet every Wednesday and roughly mirror government departments. Hence you have the Home Affairs Select Committee, the Defence Committee, the Foreign Affairs Committee and so on. In terms of function and usefulness as a leg up the ladder, they are very different.

Standing Committees will be made up of two or three ministers responsible for whatever area the Bill covers, and their Opposition shadows. The rest of the Committee composition will be left to the whips, operating through the Committee of Selection. MPs who have a particular interest or constituency link can ask to be put on, and although the numbers vary, it usually ends up with between eight and fourteen MPs on each side, and a handful of representatives from the smaller parties.

The point of the Committee Stage is to go through the Bill in painstaking detail, weeding out any inconsistencies or minor errors. The opposition parties will put down rafts of amendments whose purpose is to try to change what they feel are the most pernicious and ill-conceived elements of the particular piece of legislation in question. Government members may well put down amendments which cover a particular personal interest, but most are under instructions to sit tight and say nothing, in order to speed up the passage of the Bill, and thus can be seen catching up on their constituency mail when they think the Committee Chair's not looking. Every amendment which has been put down, whether Government or Opposition, will be debated at inordinate length.

If Stan were to feel that being on such a committee is about as exciting as spending a wet weekend at a trainspotter's convention, then he'd be absolutely right. Standing Committees can be extraordinarily boring. Some lost souls (lobbyists and special interest groups in the main, plus the odd journo) actually sit in and observe the proceedings, although watching paint dry usually has more to offer in the way of entertainment.

However, the ambitious new MP should jump at the option to get a place. The reason is simple. Standing Committees offer a unique opportunity to learn how the nitty-gritty of the legislative process works. It may be dull, but it's important. Secondly, the committee provides a first-rate opportunity for practising and sharpening political skills. The speeches and debates are conducted in much the same way as in the Chamber, but you're under nothing like the same amount of pressure. You can find your oratorical feet without feeling the world and its mother are breathing down your neck.

If you do well, it will be noted (each committee as a matter of course has a whip assigned to it). A good performance will be taken as a willingness to work hard (always respected), and possession of an eye for detail and some political nous. The Party Leader isn't going to call up and congratulate you, but you can be hopeful that the whips will have dusted off your file and written the word 'promising' against your name.

Select Committees are an altogether different thing. Set up to investigate various aspects of government departmental practice and legislation, they frequently deal in controversy, and as a consequence command a fair amount of press attention. Recent Select Committees have covered the Maxwell pension fraud, the Iraqi super-gun affair and the pricing of compact discs. They can summon people to appear before them, including ministers, senior civil servants and members of the public. At the end of a process of interrogation and taking of evidence, the committee will then produce a report. Although the committees have an inbuilt Government majority, they are frequently very critical of Government misdeeds, and many ministers have had a squirmingly unpleasant time in front of them.

Backbenchers are always very keen to get a place. For a start, proceedings are televised, which is always good news, and there's the very real feeling of power which being on a Select Committee can confer, as you summon the haughty top brass to appear before you. Then there are the interrogations. You may walk into committee room eleven a humble Opposition backbencher, but once you get behind the semicircular line of desks, and fix your gimlet eyes on the hapless minister or Permanent Secretary who has been dragged before you, you undergo a transformation. No longer Stan Bonky, you become Perry Mason, possessed of infallible logic, rapier wit and a sardonic, mocking laugh.

You will notice with pleasure that there is a faint sheen of sweat on the victim's brow, that he is wriggling in the chair and that his eyes are darting around the room. You will lean back, steeple your fingers, raise an eyebrow, and begin. 'Minister, are you really asking us to believe . . . ?' is always a nice start. Or 'I would be most interested to hear your explanation, Minister, for the following'. Or anything along these lines really, as long as it's delivered in tones of breathtaking arrogance, much like a very scholarly headteacher talking to a particularly stupid and grubby child. The minister will absolutely loathe you for it, but who cares? It will look tremendous on TV.

Once again the whips will be keeping a judicious eye on proceedings. If you succeed in making a mug of a minister, they will be pleased. They will pull your file out of the drawer and next to 'promising' they will scrawl 'bright'.

Joining the Elite – the Front Bench

So you've done your bit on the respective committees. In addition to this you will have made strenuous attempts to grovel in the many and various ways that are open to you. Stan will have lost no opportunity to praise the Party Leader, both privately and publicly. He will have made himself useful by supporting the party line in any number of debates, no matter how dismal and late-night those debates may have been. If lucky enough to come high in the draw for Questions to departmental ministers, or to the Prime Minister, he will have checked with the Shadow Cabinet member or the Leader's Office about what to say before getting up in the Chamber. Finally, when the yearly elections for the Labour Party Leader and Deputy Leader come around, Stan will be one of the first to nominate the present incumbents, notwithstanding the fact that they are under no threat whatsoever. There are some forelock-tuggers who are shameless enough to deliver their ballot papers into the hands of the Leader's PPS, but this degree of self-abasement is embarrassing rather than effective. It is hard to feel gratitude towards a doormat.

The idea is to make it plain that you're on the right side, and to appear perky, intelligent and keen. You must, however, tread carefully, and try to retain at least the appearance of a smidgen of self respect. If you go for the out and out grovel, you will seem laughable rather than laudable, and become what is commonly known as a toerag.

The Labour Party holds its Shadow Cabinet Elections in October/November. Once the results are announced, and the shadow portfolios allocated, there follow a few days during which those elected will discuss the make-up of their front bench teams with the Party Leader. Depending on the size of department, each Shad Cab member will have between two and five people on his team. This is a period of intense negotiation. There are probably twenty or so people who stand out as being good. Everyone on the Shad Cab would like to have them on board. After that there are a few people who are worthy and reasonably talented, often hard-working and good team players. Occasional personal animosity or political disagreement aside, there is never much trouble in persuading the Shad Cab elect to take them on. Then there are the others, a handful of people who were on the front bench last year, and were so crap, idle and irritating that no one wants to touch them.

Why not just dump them then, you may naively ask? Well, some will be dumped, but others are unfortunately undumpable, because they represent a certain strand of political thinking, or because it would cause a fuss in the press, or simply because the individual concerned knows where too many of the bodies are buried. There will be much argument about who should go and who should stay, and much horse trading about who gets stuck with the worst of the incumbent donkeys. At the end of this tortuous process there may be four or five empty places. Before this juncture is reached, Stan should have taken care to single out a couple of established Shad Cab members and to put a great deal of thought, time and energy into sucking up to them.

If he's done a good job, Gordon Brown or Robin Cook will say at this juncture, 'Well, I've got a spare place on my team, what about giving Stan a go?' John Smith, having heard nothing bad about him in the course of the year, and musing over his file marked 'promising' and 'bright', will acquiesce.

After an agonising week of waiting by a phone that never

rings, Stan will suddenly leap like a scalded cat as his researcher tells him that the Leader's Office is on the phone. It won't of course be John Smith himself – Stan isn't important enough for that – but a member of the Leader's Office will explain to Stan that John would like to see him, 5.30 pm today, okay? Stan will have barely stammered out his grateful thanks before the phone goes down. There are, after all, seventy-odd more calls to get through.

At 5.25 pm Stan will walk out of the Chamber, past the Speaker's Chair, through the double doors and down the long straight corridor which leads to the Leader of the Opposition's offices. Farting with excitement and smiling nervously at the various members of staff he encounters, he will climb the narrow stairs to John's personal office. He will start to twitch a bit as John's secretary asks him to take a seat, and then finally, he will be summoned into the inner sanctum. A short chat will ensue. After being congratulated on his incisive performance on the Home Affairs Select Committee, Stan will be offered the most junior of the front bench positions on the Environment Team. He should accept with becoming gratitude, talk briefly (very) about his abiding interest in housing and local authorities and then leave. He will keep to a dignified walk until getting past the double doors at the end of the corridor, after which it's permissible to run, skip and jump and head straight for the Members' Bar to receive congratulations and order big drinks all round.

Shadow Cabinet

Until the rules were altered, providing for a quota of women to be elected, most MPs spent a couple of years or so on the front bench before having the temerity to put themselves up for the Shadow Cabinet Elections. Only other Labour MPs (collectively referred to as the Parliamentary Labour Party or PLP) are eligible to vote. The PLP has been called 'the most sophisticated electorate in the world'. This is roughly akin to calling Jeffrey Archer 'the best novelist in the world'. Both statements are debatable.

If you are good at your front bench job, perform impressively in the House, get in the press a lot, and start to build a reputation as a rising star, it is time for the Shadow Cabinet. However, this is not the end of the story. People get elected to the Shad Cab for a variety of reasons. Some get on because they are quite obviously very talented. Some get on because they are widely popular, and all their friends vote for them, and some get on because they manipulate the voting system with consummate skill.

Each member of the PLP votes for eighteen people, and four of those votes have to be cast for women MPs, or else the ballot paper is rendered invalid. MPs vote according to a bewildering number of different factors. Politically speaking, there is the hard left Campaign Group. Numerically insignificant (about 30 MPs), they purport to vote *en bloc*, and tend to be very picky about the candidates they'll endorse. Over the years very few of their own number have ever made it, but their support for outside candidates has often been crucial, the more so for never being made public. Tribune is supposedly the Labour Party's soft left grouping, but nowadays is absolutely huge, and includes just about anyone else who wants to be a member, having moved a very long way from the great days of Nye Bevan, Ian Mikardo and Michael Foot. In the old days there used to be a Tribune slate for the Shadow Cabinet, and great attempts were made to achieve a common slate with the Campaign Group, but such was the climate of comradely mistrust that it never worked. Tribune no longer produces a slate, and the group makes little pretence of voting as a block.

There are of course other political undercurrents at work: pro and anti Europeans, electoral reformers, trade union stalwarts and one member one voters. The problem with all this is that you lose as much as you gain. If you win the admiration of one side, you can be sure that no one on the other side will countenance you, and of course they tend to cancel each other out.

The second set of important allegiances within the Labour Party are the regional groupings to which each MP belongs by virtue of constituency. Some groups, Scottish, Welsh and

Northern & Yorkshire, have a strong and cohesive identity. Even better, they have lots of members. An MP standing for the Shadow Cabinet from any of these groups can rely on a very useful amount of votes.

Denied any helpful regional or political back-up, the thing to do is to start electioneering the day after the previous year's vote is announced. This involves showing how hard you work. Any serious would-be Shadow Cabinet Member will have long since got the names and addresses of every member of the PLP on computerised sticky labels. These will have been further broken down into regional groupings, women and, if the MP concerned is a real worker, special interests. These labels will be used for monthly mass mail-outs of surveys, policy documents and handily customised press releases, so the recipient can just fill in his or her name and bang it out to the local newspaper.

The potential Shadow Cabinet Member will also put aside a not inconsiderable amount of money for an entertainment budget. It is commonly agreed that in 1992 one MP was successful simply because he had bought so many drinks and slapped so many backs. This may sound very far-fetched, but in a place as cut-throat as the House of Commons, a little camaraderie goes a long way. For example, Barry Jones, MP for Alyn and Deeside, previously Shadow Secretary of State for Wales, got voted on year after year in a gravity-defying display. Barry had a simple secret. He was nice to people. Other MPs were so stunned and shocked by such unprecedented displays of human warmth that they couldn't help but vote for him. Admittedly Barry's niceness was somewhat specialised. Known as 'Jones the Note', he kept up an endless stream of billets doux all year long. Suppose you were a new MP, and you made your first three-second and rather undistinguished appearance on the Six o'clock News. The following day a hand-written missive would arrive via the House of Commons internal post. It would be from Barry, telling you that you were marvellous, had a real talent for television and were definitely front bench material. The new MP was naturally chuffed to bits, and that was one vote in the bag for Bazza.

If you're going to do this sort of thing you have to be good at it. Barry Jones was a master. Not so the would-be Shadow Cabinet Member who wrote to all sixty nine new Labour MPs in the summer of 1992, congratulating the newcomers on their 'exceptionally fine' maiden speeches. Not only did many of them compare notes and find that they had identical letters, but some were more than a little confused, as they had not yet made their maiden speeches. It is almost pointless to record that the Member in question failed abysmally.

Even when you finally make it on to the Shadow Cabinet there's more agony to come. Your every summer holiday will be blighted by the dreaded October elections. If you came in the bottom half of the poll last year, you will be terrified of being knocked off; if you came in the top half you will be terrified of sliding down the ratings. Your arms will be sore from back slapping, and your jaw will ache from hours of smiling at your colleagues, their staff, families and anybody else you think may remotely influence the outcome of the vote. For the Shadow Cabinet many are called, but few are chosen.

Going to the Top with the Tories

How to become a Tory grandee? How do you get ahead and get a job in the party of the establishment? In some respects things are not so very different from the other parties, except for one thing. The Conservatives have a healthy contempt for the democratic process, which makes the life of Stanley Brinsley-Bonky that much easier. Unlike his opposite number in the Labour Party, he will not have to go through the tortuous process of trying to persuade a hundred odd of his parliamentary colleagues to vote for him. If the Prime Minister likes him, it doesn't matter what the rest of Stanley's colleagues think, because the Prime Minister will give him a job.

The upside of this is that there is no need to be outrageously nice to battalions of half-wit MPs. No need to spend hours talking about how North Sea oil properly belongs to Scotland in order to get the fifty odd comrades north of the border to vote for you in the Shadow Cabinet Elections. Instead you can suggest that if Scotland is really so keen on independence, why not start rebuilding Hadrian's Wall now? This cheerful and carefree trampling over the sensitivities of your colleagues will make for a happier and longer life, and provide you with hours of harmless fun at their expense.

However, attempting to become a 'Top Tory Nob' – to borrow a phrase from the tabloids – isn't all claret and cigars. In the Conservative Party, appointments are made on the basis of patronage and preferment. The result of this, is what politics students are apt to call 'clientelism'. The would-be junior minister is a client or supplicant, every well-rehearsed move is made entirely for the benefit of the core command, that is the Prime Minister, the Chief Whip and a handful of particularly influential Cabinet Ministers and close advisors. Because the targets for grovelling are so restricted, and so universally acknowledged, the intensity of your self abasement has to be something really special to warrant any notice at all.

As a newcomer there is one watchword to remember – LOYALTY. It still seems to be the attribute most admired in the Tory Party, far in excess of intelligence, diligence or morality. At the bottom of their hearts, mainstream, conscientious Tories couldn't give a toss about ideas or beliefs or any of that crap. What they really believe in is their inalienable right to run the country, however badly. Very occasionally a division may occur in the ranks, as on the question of Europe, but this tends to be the exception rather than the rule. Having your own ideas, asking difficult questions, or indeed thinking very much at all, is pretty well frowned upon in respectable Conservative circles.

As a new backbencher you will, above all things, do what you're told. This is passive loyalty: always voting with the Government, turning up when needed, doing the business on Standing Committees, and trying your best to defend Government personnel appearing before the Select Committee of which you're a member. This accomplished, the next stage is to pass on to active loyalty. This involves regular press denunciations of any supposed rebels, ferocious counter-attacks against the Opposition, and losing no opportunity to tell the nation what an exceptionally gifted, able, nay visionary, leader the current Prime Minister really is. This is where devices such as the Brown Nose Question can come in very handy. The BNQ is a variant of the PMQ, and its proper usage goes something like this. The draw for Prime Minister's Questions is published. Your name stands at number six. You won't definitely get called, but you have a fair chance. Because you are a truly loyal backbencher, you will immediately ring Number 10, explain your position in the draw and ask what the PM would like you to say. The burning issue of the day will be tackled by a colleague who has come higher in the draw. It is suggested, however, that you could call attention to the marvellous successes of the government's Healthy Eating campaign, whose winning slogan *'Don't cash yer chips in'* is a wonderful example of the PM's effective common touch. You gladly comply, and are faxed sheaves of statistics, pointing to the decline in heart disease in the north of England and the plummeting sales of lard in all major food retailers. Well prepared, you enter the fray.

'Could I ask my Right Honourable Friend', you will cry, 'to join with me in celebrating the success of his marvellous health initiative. Is it not the case that, because of the Prime Minister's personal interest in health promotion and the *Chips In* campaign, the NHS is estimated to have saved over 2.5 *billion* (always emphasise the *billion*) pounds, and that British people are living for up to five years longer?'

This is not a bad effort, and the PM will duly get up and thank you for your very pertinent question, adding that he is pleased to report that the £2.5 *billion* has been reallocated within the NHS to build a new children's unit in the East Midlands. There is, however, more to be done with this opportunity if you've the mind to do it. For example, if you are cultivating an Opposition-bashing-thug persona you would approach the whole thing differently. Once on your feet, you would congratulate the PM on his slim figure and vigorous health. 'Isn't it a pity,' you would snarl, 'that the Leader of the Opposition hasn't endorsed the Government's outstanding *Chips* campaign? Wouldn't the Prime Minister agree that that lot over there have already had their chips? They've been battered, and just like the salmon, they're on the rocks.' This astonishingly witty sally will make the PM laugh, and the troops will love you for it. It is, though, as well to remember that if you have any pretensions to intellectualism or rationality such lines are not for you. Which is why they are so often employed by David Evans, the hard-line, right-wing MP for Welwyn and Hatfield.

Edwina Currie, MP for Derbyshire South, probably wins the fiercely contested prize for most grovelling BNQ, put to the Mad Axewoman of Finchley. Could she tell the Prime Minister, said Edwina brightly, what a lovely outfit she was wearing, and what a particularly fine example she set to the rest of the country? This really is the incisive cutting edge of political debate.

The final thing to remember about the whole loyalty thing is to whom you're supposed to be loyal. Most people are uncomplicated enough happily to accept the current incumbent, and bring all their energies to bear on sucking up to him or her. Occasionally there are far-sighted or machiavellian souls who have an entirely different agenda. Still loyal to the last regime, or hopefully preparing the ground for the one to come, they make a bloody nuisance of themselves by twitting the great and the good, an activity known as standing outside the tent and pissing in. David Evans made it clear in a recent speech (7/6/93) that he was less than impressed by the government's record on law and order. 'In my view,' he said, 'that problem has been caused by a succession of weak-kneed, pathetic Home Secretaries – not least the immediate past incumbent, the present Chancellor.' In case you're wondering, Mr Evans is nominally on the same side as the weak-kneed and pathetic individuals he describes. If he thinks Kenneth Clarke is indecisive, what the hell does he make of John Major? But then, political consistency has never been one of Mr Evans' worries. Philip Oppenheim MP is another right-winger and Thatcher loyalist, but of a far more sophisticated kind. Remembering Michael Heseltine's famous 'I will intervene before breakfast' speech at the 1992 Conservative Party Conference, Mr Oppenheim put down a Question to the would-be interventionist President of the Board of Trade. 'How many meetings had he had with business men before 8.30 am in the last month' he asked disingenuously. El Presidente was not amused. 'I have had no such meetings,' the answer read. (Hansard 17/3/93)

Although such excursions are amusing enough, they are mere distractions to the business in hand. Suppose Stanley Brinsley-Bonky keeps his nose clean, sucks up to the PM shamelessly and finally gets offered a job, what then?

Ministering to the Afflicted

Being a junior minister, like being a junior anything, is a bit of a duff job. Your civil servants will load you with work enclosed in the ubiquitous red boxes. These caskets of reinforced cardboard, embossed with royal coats of arms and the ministerial title, will begin to take on a horrible significance in your life. Much like God, they will be omnipresent. You will take them home every night, spend two hours wading through them, take them back, where they will be packed up again. At weekends you will be loaded down with four or five of them. Civil servants dislike ministers who 'interfere' with the smooth running of the country. The red boxes are a handy device for tying them down and keeping them out of trouble. The idea is that the minister becomes so exhausted and overloaded with a myriad of detail that he or she is quite unable to put their mind to larger and more important matters. Any minister who shows an unhealthy desire to know what's actually going on in the department, much worse attempt to control or change it, will immediately find that their red box count multiplies. Similarly, a lazy and pliant minister will be accommodated with a lighter burden, for the civil servants are quite happy to take care of everything, as long as the minister has the good sense to keep out of the way.

Being a junior minister is all about making the life of the boss (the Secretary of State) as painless as humanly possible. If your department is getting flak, you should try to take the majority of it. If the boss has taken a decision costing thousands of jobs and laying economic waste to vast stretches of the country, then it is your job to go on *Newsnight* and defend what you quite possibly thought to be a ludicrous and ill-conceived idea in the first place. You may have argued vehemently against it in departmental meetings, but it will be you twitching miserably in the leather chair dealing with Mr Paxman at his most righteous and scathing. Likewise you will be the one sent to 'reassure' the redundant workforce and devastated communities that the Government's urban aid programme will be just the ticket to set things right. Conversely, if your department has some great triumph such as a huge and unexpected boost in the monthly trade figures, for example, you won't get near the TV screen. Oh no; you'll be sat at home with the red boxes watching the boss lap up the congratulations.

Whilst labouring in this political salt mine, the other thing constantly to bear in mind is that junior ministers, much like children, should be seen and not heard. The very worst thing you can possibly do is speak out of turn or say anything remotely embarrassing to the Government of which you are now a member. This will be seized on by the press as a 'Ministerial Gaffe'. The opposition will happily quote you ad nauseam and the PM, the Cabinet and most particularly your own boss will be absolutely furious with you, as they spend days trying to undo the damage caused by your big gob.

Cabinet Pudding

Getting in the Cabinet is where it's really at in terms of career advancement in British politics. Opportunities arise when the Government has a reshuffle, which is politico-speak for sacking some people and moving others to different jobs. Reshuffles frequently happen in the summer, although they can theoretically take place at any time at all. They are often heralded by weeks of speculation in the press, sometimes inspired by Downing Street, as out-of-control rumours and offhand remarks are recycled by lobby journalists, to appear in the following day's newspapers as cast-iron probabilities. For the anxious minister it can be a very trying time. Are you on for promotion? The sack? Or – worst of all possible worlds – a sideways move to one of Whitehall's graveyard departments? When the Chief Whip tells you that the Prime Minister wishes to see you, your heart will leap. If he's bothering to see Stanley Brinsley-Bonky, Minister of State for the Environment, personally, then it must be promotion. You're right, it's the Big C. The Cabinet! Half an hour later you walk out of Downing Street to smile and wave to the press. You are now Secretary of State for Wales!

A Labour Leader once said that if any Labour MP specialised in science, then said MP would eventually find himself on the Labour front bench due to the party's lack of expertise in this particular area. Likewise if any Tory MP possesses enough intelligence to pick his nose and read Hansard at the same time, providing he can prove that his granny once went to Llandudno on a day trip, he will find himself Secretary of State for Wales. Welsh Tories are a rare and dying breed. In the old days it was an accepted convention that to be Secretary of State for Wales, it was necessary to be Welsh. Unfortunately there are no longer enough Welsh Conservatives to go round and this rule has become increasingly loosely interpreted, as No. 10 becomes more and more desperate to find somebody (anybody) to fill the gap. One Welsh Minister, Sir Wyn Roberts MP, appears to have a job for life, having been appointed to his post by Margaret Thatcher back in 1979. Fourteen years on, and he's still there, and likely to remain so until he drops, being the only living example of a Welsh-speaking Tory MP.

Running a ministerial department brings its own interesting challenges. There's the autumn spending round, preceding the new unified November Budget. This is where each individual spending ministry (which means practically all of them) put their bids in to the Treasury for the money they need for the coming year. This exercise is overseen by the Chief Secretary to the Treasury, who is also a member of the Cabinet, and a reasonably senior one at that. The Chief Secretary's main aim in life is to make sure no one spends any money at all. In political terms, money to spend almost exactly equates to prestige and popularity, so a great deal of lively discussion goes on, which usually results in the smaller and less politically sensitive departments getting well and truly done over at the expense of the big boys with the muscle. This will be your first real test as Secretary of State. If you get turned over by the Treasury and limp back to your Department with a black eye and a pittance, your civil servants will hate and despise you for it (because it affects their prestige as well) and you will spend the next year making hugely unpopular cuts.

The other thing about being a Secretary of State is that you are actually expected to *do* something. This can all come as a bit of a shock. You've been happily jogging along for years, secure in the knowledge that you were only obeying orders, and then suddenly this great big untidy bundle of responsibility is dropped squarely in your lap. You're in charge, and the buck has well and truly stopped. People are looking to you for leadership, ideas and, most pertinently, to *Initiate Legislation*.

Legislation is the politician's *raison d'être*. It's what it's all about. You know, putting Bills before Parliament, passing laws, *changing things*. The trouble is that all this legislating business is easier said than done. To start with, you've got to decide what you want to do. Sat there in his departmental office in Cardiff, Stanley Brinsley-Bonky will chew his biro and stare out of the window hopelessly waiting for inspiration to strike, and it can't be any old inspiration either. Firstly, it's got to be within the remit of his department; secondly, it preferably has to have no – and by no we mean *no* – cost implications whatsoever; thirdly, it should avoid embarrassing political fall-out, in terms of lost jobs or revenues, or upsetting powerful sectional or lobbying interests; fourthly, it should be such that it gathers significant support from other members of the Cabinet; fifthly, (pay attention, most important) it should at least have been alluded to in the election manifesto, fit in with the overall Government programme and please the PM; sixthly, it must marry into the overall legislative schedule. Easy, really, isn't it? Reading down this list you suddenly understand how ministers can come up with schemes such as the poll tax and care in the community. By the time you've jumped over or run round all the other hurdles in your path, the simple problem that the whole thing was a lunatic scheme in the first place seems hardly to matter. In addition to this you will be plagued by your civil servants, who will place before you pet prospective Bills which the previous Secretary of State laughed to scorn, and which they will now try to bounce off you.

Once the miserable Secretary of State has dreamt up a passable piece of legislation (for sake of argument the *National Parks (Wales) Privatisation Bill*) then comes the next test. For some bizarre reason Bills are like ships, 'piloted' and occasionally 'steered' on their progress through the Commons and the Lords, at the end of which they receive the Royal Assent and become Acts. It is true that sometimes the ship bears an uncomfortable resemblance to the *Titanic* rather than the *Ark Royal*, but in essence that's the point. You are the captain. If she goes down with all hands on deck, and the band playing *Land of Hope and Glory*, it will be seen as completely your fault. The idea is to keep a sharp look-out for icebergs.

By the time you've finished traipsing through the First Reading (entirely formal, lasting only as long as it takes to read out the title of the Bill), Second Reading (torture and argy-bargy in the Commons, involving an exhausting and prolonged performance at the despatch box), Committee Stage (more torture, tedious nitty-gritty, which will force you to know the Bill backwards, forwards and sideways, and worse still to realise that it's actually deficient in many important respects) and Report Stage (giving the opposition yet another chance to whinge about why the Bill is so awful, you will have to produce dozens of amendments in order to rectify all the deficiencies of intent, purpose and drafting. Come the Third Reading (more or less a formality, by now you'll be totally demob happy), your life will not be worth living. Throughout this grim process you will have been sustained by the loyal payroll vote and the whips, who will ensure a majority for every one of the dozens of divisions you will endure, notwithstanding the fact that few of your supporters will have even the foggiest idea just what they're voting for, or indeed against. You will be ecstatic to see the back of the hated Bill as it makes its progress to the Lords, where the Peers will get their chance to repeat the entire malarky. If fate has singled you out for special punishment, it might, just might, be amended by the Lords and sent back to the Commons, in which case you'd have to heave yourself to your feet and go through the same arguments all over again. By the time the Bill receives Royal Assent, you'll probably be so completely sick of the entire concept of Welsh parks, private or otherwise, that you'll be imperilling your entire ministerial career by crafting your next piece of legislation, entitled *National Parks (Wales) Napalm and Carpet Bombing Bill*.

One final word of warning – the higher up the greasy pole you climb, the further you have to fall, and the more unedifying a view you present to those shinning up beneath you. Cabinet Ministers don't have friends, they just know people who want their jobs. Before bracing yourself for the perilous ascent up the career ladder of politics, you may reflect that there are other, perhaps more rewarding, ways of spending your time in the House of Commons.

Chapter Four

How to Go Too Far and Get Away with It

When Sebastian Coe was first elected, he took the precaution of ringing up a couple of Tory elder statesmen to ask what it was going to be like what he got to the hallowed portals of Parliament. 'Don't worry dear boy,' they replied. 'It's exactly like your old school.' When he finally arrived in the Commons, Seb could in fact see very little resemblance to the concrete and graffiti of Tapton Secondary School, Sheffield. But of course that wasn't the sort of school he meant.

In other respects, however, the Tory grandees were dead right. The House of Commons is not at all unlike a large public school. It has its teachers, prefects and uniforms, its completely inedible school dinners. Like most schools, it has its bad boys, always bending the rules, forever on the brink of expulsion. Some get away with it, some go too far, and after innumerable warnings are finally sent down.

Many people seem to think that the scenes of noise and bluster witnessed in the Chamber are a modern innovation, that like the crime statistics, MPs' bad behaviour has got much worse. Sadly, this just isn't true. MPs have never behaved well, but if anything things have actually improved in recent years.

The Good Old Days

The sort of people who tell you that things were better when Britain had an Empire, and the local bobby would get off his bike and give little Johnny a clip round the ear if he caught him up to no good, will also tell you that MPs ain't what they used to be.

There is a stubborn belief in a parliamentary golden age, when MPs were gentlemen, wore nice hats, and had impeccable manners; a time when British fair play was the order of the day, and opponents were heard in respectful silence.

This is bollocks. The House of Commons is by nature a rowdy bear garden, but in comparison with some of their predecessors, today's MPs are a bunch of wimps.

People who go to the House for the day, and are shown around on a guided tour by their MP, are usually surprised when they enter the Chamber. It is much smaller than expected, and it is noticeable that when leaning on their respective despatch boxes to speak, the Prime Minister and the Leader of the Opposition are less than a yard apart. Now it isn't necessary to pay a firm of American consultants $200,000 to explain that, 'Hey, in terms of interpersonal and psychological interface, the physical logistics of the Chamber of the House of Commons lend themselves to a total conflict scenario!' Broadly speaking, if you are sitting bang opposite someone who contradicts everything you say, shouts abuse and, when leaning forward, is only a couple of feet away from poking your eye out, it's guaranteed to make you lose your temper.

Almost every other parliament and legislature in the world has got the point of all this, and arranged their seating in the round, thus making it impossible to scream threats and vilification directly into someone's face, and undermining the oppositional and confrontational nature of debate. Good Old Blighty, however, has clung firmly to tradition, and kept the 'them and us' arrangement. Thus from time immemorial, the House of Commons has been the scene of grown men indulging in tempter tantrums that would shame the average two-year-old. It's understandable to say 'they should know better', but it's far less easy to keep cool when you're actually there.

As if in recognition of this, another feature of the Chamber is the two red parallel lines down the carpet, drawn about two feet in front of the Government and Opposition benches.

These are the 'sword lines', and date from the days when MPs regularly turned up wearing their swords. The lines are approximately two and a half sword-lengths apart, and you are not supposed to cross them. The idea was that when things hotted up, they would prevent Honourable Members running each other through in a fit of fury. This is allegedly the origin of the phrase 'toeing the line'. Although MPs are still legally allowed to carry swords, and have sword ribbons along with coat hangers issued when they are first elected, no one has been seen doing an Errol Flynn in the Chamber recently. The lines, however, remain, as a sort of symbolic separation.

If you need proof that in the House of Commons the Good Old Days never existed, it is not hard to find. Pepys writes in his *Diary* of 29 July 1667 the following description of a day in Parliament:

'To Westminster Hall, where the Hall full of people to see the issues of the day, the King being to come to speak to the House today. One extraordinary thing was this day, a man, a Quaker, came naked through the Hall, only very civilly tied about the privities to avoid scandal, and with a chafing dish of fire and brimstone burning upon his head did pass through the Hall crying "Repent! Repent!"'

The *Journals* of the Commons reveal that some problems are perennial. In February of 1692, it was 'ordered that the Ser-jeant-at-Arms do go into Westminster Hall and the several Bars to summon Members to attend the service of the House immediately'. As any Whip will tell you, little has changed. The first places the Whips look when trying to round up the stragglers for the 10 pm vote are the many and various bars of the House of Commons. This isn't because MPs are by nature dipsomaniacs – it's simply because there is sod all else to do. For example, suppose you arrived at work at 9.30 am, spent the day doing your job, hoping optimistically to be able to leave at 7pm (when the House is sitting, there is often a 7 pm vote), and then you're told by the boss, at around 4.30 pm, that you have to stay until 10 pm at least, and that there is no guarantee that you will be going home even then.

Having put in your eight hours plus of hard work, you are faced with having to hang about for a further three or four hours. If you are a mad, careerist workaholic, you then go back to your office, rejoicing in the opportunity to write two more press releases and read the circulars that everyone else threw into the bin earlier in the day. If you are genuinely interested in the matter under consideration, or a closet masochist, you will spend the three hours in the chamber, listening to your parliamentary colleagues. If you're an average member of the human race, you will retire exhausted to the bar, and slump in a corner, staring moodily into your glass and wishing you were somewhere else. I have some sympathy with the AWOL MPs in 1692. *Plus ça change . . .*

Some things *have* changed, though, and for the better. Dr Johnson's biographer, James Boswell, visited the Commons in March 1763, and wasn't very impressed. 'My respect for it was greatly abated by seeing such a tumultuous scene. A Member lying stretched out on one of the benches, while others crack nuts or eat oranges, or what ever else is in season.' Such behaviour is never seen today, as it is totally verboten to eat or drink in the Chamber, a discreet sip of water being just about permitted.

In fact, in most respects, the so-called 'golden age' of parliamentary good manners was not what it was cracked up to be. There were numerous minor outbursts and infringements. In the early 1800s one Sussex Member was so disruptive that he had to be physically removed and detained for the night. The reason for such exuberance was made clear in typical parliamentary fashion. He was not drunk, naturally, but 'was in a situation in which he could not altogether appreciate the very improper nature of his conduct'. Yes, we see. In other words, tired as a newt.

The Home Rule Bills debated in the late 19th century spawned their share of top-grade mayhem. In 1881, after a fracas about the Speaker's ruling to end the debate, twenty eight Members were suspended *en masse*. They refused to withdraw unless compelled to do so, and the Serjeant-at-Arms was duly sent for. Most yielded to a tap on the shoulder, but some were more unwilling and had to be rugby tackled and removed from the House by main force.

In terms of really outrageous behaviour, though, surely the House's finest hour came in 1893, when once more Home Rule was being debated. On 28 July the Bill had reached the last day allotted for the Committee Stage. Gladstone, very much the Grand Old Man, and edging towards his 90s, was Prime Minister. Joseph Chamberlain, although nominally of the same party, behaved rather like the Ted Heath of his day, and started his speech by complaining about the dog-like devotion of Gladstone's followers. 'If the Prime Minister says it's black, they say it is good; if white they say it is better. It is always the voice of a god. Never, since the time of Herod, has there been such slavish adulation.'

Not surprisingly, this did not go down well. Cries of 'Judas! Judas!' were taken up around the Chamber, with counter-vening shouts of 'Order! Order!' from the Tory benches. Someone with the unlikely name of Vicary Gibbs started jumping up and down with his hat on to try to call the atten-tion of the Chairman, and from there on in, things went down-hill rather quickly.

The impressively titled A S T Griffith-Boscawen, MP for Ton-bridge, gives a full account of the carnage in his memoirs entitled *Fourteen Years in Parliament* (London: 1907, John Murray). After Mr Vicary Gibbs's fruitless attempts to catch the Chairman's eye, according to A S T G-B, total chaos erupted. A pro-Nationalist MP called Mr Logan, whom A S T G-B describes as 'a somewhat aggressive Radical', rushed across from the Liberal benches and sat in the middle of the Conservative Opposition front bench. Mr Logan then pro-ceeded to argue very heatedly with the arch-Unionist, Edward Carson. 'What his (Logan's) object was, nobody could divine,' says G-B, 'but his intrusion was greatly resented by the Conservatives.' So greatly resented, in fact, it impelled the Tory on the bench directly behind to lean forward and shove Logan on to the floor. All hell immediately broke loose. The Irish Nationalists, who were seated on the Government benches and the Liberals 'rose almost as one man, and . . . rushed across the gangway towards the Conservatives, specially singling out Colonel Saunderson for attack'. What Colonel Saunderson's special crime was seems to be lost in the mists of time. Anyway he proved to be the sort of man who had built the empire, and old G-B can barely keep the panting admiration out of his voice. 'The Colonel was equal to the emergency,' we learn, and 'taking off his coat, he hit about valiantly and kept his assailants at bay.'

Whilst the Colonel was doing his thin-red-line-at-Rorke's Drift number, there were apparently 'three or four other scuffles taking place simultaneously in other parts of the Chamber.' Fortunately, 'Members were packed so closely together that they could hardly get at each other, and no real damage was done.'

Meanwhile, poor old Gladstone was still wading through his speech in the midst of this full-scale riot, presenting 'a most pitiable sight . . . standing in front of the Treasury Bench as pale as a sheet . . . while opposite him was Sir Ellis Ashmead Bartlett, wildly gesticulating, and shouting "This is all your fault." It's good to know that, in time of crisis, the House can rise above mere party division to face the oncoming storm. What a comfort Sir Ellis's words must have been.

Some semblance of order was finally restored by the appearance of the Speaker, Arthur Wellesley Peel, who, almost magically in the circumstances, managed to calm things down. A S T Griffith-Boscawen is, however, not shy in apportioning blame. His fellow Tory, Sir Ellis Ashmead Bartlett, was, we learn, 'not far from the mark' in telling Gladstone that it was all 'his fault'. But the real burden of guilt falls on the Irish Members, and the Liberals whose 'manners had been corrupted by association with them'. In a wonderfully even-handed and judicial summing up, G-B concludes that the Liberal Logan's foray on to the Conservative front bench 'can in no way be condoned', whilst the Tory who reacted by shoving Logan on to the floor was 'guilty of an error of judgement, very pardonable under the circumstances'. Quite.

When things finally calmed down, and the battered and bruised combatants of both sides went home to bed, the House of Commons' staff arrived to clear up the Chamber. Amongst the debris was found a broken bench arm, a plethora of buttons and shirt studs, and a dislodged tooth.

1893 was a lively year. On 28 July another scene occurred when Labour MP Keir Hardie voted against a motion to congratulate the Duchess of York on the birth of a son. Complaining that the resolution lifted 'to an importance which it did not deserve an event of everyday occurrence', Keir Hardie reminded the House that over two hundred men had died in the recent Welsh mining disaster, and proposed that the Government should use the opportunity to express their condolences with the relatives of 'those who were lying stiff and stark in a Welsh valley'. Uproar ensued, and a *West Ham Herald* reporter described the scene as follows: 'I've been in a wild beast show at feeding time. I've been at a football match when a referee gave a wrong decision . . . but in all my natural life I have never witnessed a scene like this.' But it's good to be able to report that good taste and common sense won the day. The Question was put twice to the House and on each occasion 'Mr Keir Hardie was the only dissident'.

Celtic affairs have always had the power to provoke high passion in the House of Commons, and it is probably fair to say that Scottish MPs operate on as short a fuse as any. Matters got sadly out of hand in 1931 when a Glasgow Labour MP named McGovern stood up at Question Time to press the Secretary of State for Scotland to order the release of two men who had been sentenced for taking part in demonstrations on Glasgow Green without the requisite public permit.

Fairly predictably, Mr McGovern didn't receive a satisfactory answer. He then refused point blank to resume his seat in the Chamber. Eventually the Speaker named him, and the then Prime Minister, Ramsay MacDonald, moved that McGovern be suspended, which was carried by three hundred and fifteen votes to sixteen. The Scottish MP still refused to leave, and the Serjeant-at-Arms was called, arriving with four henchmen for the task in hand. As they tried to manhandle the resisting MP out of the Chamber, McGovern's colleagues intervened. What followed was described by *The Times* (3 July 1931 & passim) as 'an ugly scene of violence', as 'a swaying group of struggling men moved slowly towards the door'. Just as McGovern was grappled clear of the Chamber door, Mr Beckett, one of the MPs who had gone to his aid, was knocked down in the struggle and got back on his feet in a 'dishevelled and excited' state, after which he walked 'slowly back to his seat' rubbing his arm and leg.

The Times took an extremely firm line on such behaviour. 'There is nothing brave or clever about it,' intoned The Thunderer. Mr McGovern, it was felt, was 'childishly incompetent to control himself' and, worse still, was bringing into disrepute a 'system of party politics (which) for all its imperfections (deals) with a great Empire'.

There was, however, a silver lining to this particular parliamentary dark cloud. In the cold light of day, the rebellious Members saw things rather differently, and made the sort of apology that would have left Mother Teresa standing in the humility stakes. The Prime Minister was quite overcome by the emotion of it all. The whole House, he said, would be 'very gratified' by the apologies made and especially, 'If I may say so, (by) the beautiful, sincere and frank statement made by the Hon. Member for Bridgeton (Mr Maxton), (which) might be taken as a model'. The ducking and diving Mr Beckett hadn't done quite so well, and the PM felt his apology could have been 'a little more thorough and wholehearted', but it was clear, as Lloyd George said, that 'the right course has been taken, and the sooner this disagreeable incident is forgotten the better'.

The Thirties saw one other exciting incident, when Commander Bower (where have all these military folk gone to? The place used to be infested with them), the Unionist MP for Cleveland, told the Labour MP Manny Shinwell to 'Go Back To Poland!' This remark was, of course, entirely irrelevant to the business in hand, but it was enough for the diminutive Manny, later Lord, Shinwell, who crossed the floor of the House and hit Bower round the head so hard that he permanently damaged the MP's hearing. Shinwell then invited Bower (a naval boxing heavyweight) 'outside', but the Unionist plainly recognised a potential good hiding when he saw one and refused to budge. Rather bizarrely, the two men later became firm friends.

Crimes of Passion

Compared with such splendid examples of utter mayhem, modern age parliamentary misbehaviour all seems a bit pallid and limp-wristed. The nearest we've got to the full-blooded physical riots described above was the occasion shortly after Bloody Sunday (January 1972, when fourteen unarmed civilians were shot dead by British paratroopers in Derry in Ireland). Bernadette Devlin was then the MP for Mid Ulster, and a native of Derry City. Previously a student leader of the growing equal rights movement in Northern Ireland, she was by far the youngest Member of the House of Commons, and was obviously completely unaware of the rules regarding discussion of 'Tragic Events'. On these occasions the House is supposed to Be-At-Its-Best, and Speak-With-One-Voice. A tone of elevated seriousness is *de rigueur*, and phrases such as 'unavoidable tragedy', 'heart goes out to the innocent victims', 'firm action to ensure no repetition' abound. Unfortunately, no one had told Bernadette. Shocked and furious after the murder of fourteen people from the town she had been born and brought up in, she was quite unable to appreciate the political gravitas of the situation.

Her irritation increased when it became clear that the then Speaker, Selwyn Lloyd, quite disgracefully had absolutely no intention of calling her to speak, despite her being the only Member who had actually been present at the incident. When it became obvious he was about to close the debate, Bernadette boiled over. Having called Reggie Maudling a liar and a 'murdering hypocrite', she took matters into her own hands and, in the words of *The Times*, 'strode across the floor of the House to the Government Front Bench and punched Mr Maudling'. She rather luckily got two for the price of one, hitting Ted Heath in the mouth with the backswing. Some Labour MPs followed her across, and began trading punches with their Conservative opposites, and a general mêlée broke out, until the whips intervened and escorted Bernadette out of the Chamber. Tony Benn famously described her attack on Maudling (not the most alert of individuals) as the nearest anyone's ever come to waking him up.

Another parliamentary *crime passionnel* involved none other than Michael Heseltine, who, in his day, could give anyone a run for their money in the enraged loony stakes.

The incident occurred in May 1976, when the then Labour Government were trying to get their Bill on the Nationalisation of Aircraft and Shipbuilding through the House. Numbers were enormously tight, and the tension rose high when the tellers came back after the first vote on the Bill and announced a tie, three hundred and three votes for, three hundred and three votes against. In line with precedent, the Speaker, George Thomas, used his casting vote for the Government, which then won the motion by one vote. Things were hotting up, as everyone present realised that if the second vote was tied, precedence would mean that the Speaker would this time vote with the Opposition, and the Bill would then, to all practical effect, be lost.

The Labour whips, however, had a trick up their sleeve. There is an arrangement in the House of Commons called 'pairing', whereby an MP may be absent from an important vote, by virtue of pairing up with an MP from the opposite side, thus ensuring the lost votes cancel each other out. In terms of serious illness or ministerial business overseas or whatever, this is obviously a sensible and useful arrangement, and is sorted out via what are called 'the usual channels'.

Fifteen minutes after the first tied vote, the tellers came back to announce the second. The Government had won by three hundred and four to three hundred and three votes. Ecstatic Labour MPs burst out singing The Red Flag, and, in the words of *The Times* (28/5/76) 'Mr Michael Heseltine, Opposition front bench spokesman on industry, seized the mace . . . and behind the bar of the House blows were exchanged. Elder statesmen like Mr Geoffrey Rippon abused the Government backbenchers around him in the roughest words.' The Speaker had to suspend the House for twenty minutes until everyone calmed down.

Hezza had in fact done more than merely seize the Mace, having swung it around his head in an athletic, not to say primordial fashion, which gained him the lasting sobriquet of 'Tarzan'.

The reason for the fury on the Conservative benches was that it seemed that the Labour whips had found the extra, and winning, vote by breaking the pair arrangement, and Tom Pendry, supposedly a paired Labour MP, had walked through the Government lobby. But this was denied by the Labour Party.

The sound and fury of this high-octane occasion has an interesting footnote. A Mr Peter Fry, the Conservative MP for Wellingborough, had, in spite of three warnings, left earlier for a holiday in Corfu, thus depriving his party of the vital extra vote which would have defeated the Government. When the press finally caught up with the errant MP in sunny Corfu, and regaled him with stories of his party's defeat, the consequential crowd violence and disaster, all of which could, it's fair to say, be laid directly at his door, Mr Fry showed that he had not lost his clear political perspective. 'I am shattered,' he said, and what's more, 'I shall not enjoy my holiday at all now.' It is impossible to say too much about Mr Fry's unselfish and deeply responsible approach.

Liars, Murderers and Perverts

Use of 'unparliamentary language' has claimed a fair few number of victims. Tam Dalyell got chucked out twice for saying Margaret Thatcher had told an 'indefensible lie' over the sinking of the *Belgrano* (12/11/87 & 25/7/88). Ken Livingstone (25/1/88) called the Attorney General an 'accomplice to murder' when discussing the Stalker Affair, and got shown the door for his pains. Ken's trouble is that he needs to stop hedging his bets; he should come straight out and just say what he means. In similar vein, Brian Sedgemore (11/11/85) got the order of the boot for suggesting the Chancellor was 'perverting the course of justice'. In an unparalleled display of parliamentary high-mindedness, Brian explained that his 'constituents expected (him) to call Ministers to account, and to do so without fear or favour. . . . I should like to take the easy way out – the coward's way – and withdrawn, but . . . I cannot do so. The public outside expect the truth!' It's speeches like this one which put the Great back in Great Britain.

Carpe Diem – Squirts and Shits

Opportunities to insult your opponents don't grow on trees. Showing that for the real devotee, opportunities for rudeness exist where others would have never dreamt of even trying, Dennis Skinner worked himself into a lather over the emotive question of the Common Agricultural Policy and dioxin levels. It was a heroic performance, which came to a premature end when he got his marching orders for describing the Minister, John Selwyn Gummer, as 'this little squirt' (2/7/92). Which may remind us of George Foulkes's (Labour MP for Carrick, Cumnock and Doon Valley) description of Douglas Hogg, the then Trade and Industry Minister, as an 'arrogant little shit'. When asked by the Speaker to withdraw the offensive word, George said he was happy to do so, but which word: Arrogant? Little? Or shit?

Spoilers

Much beloved by the smaller parties, this tactic offers unparalleled opportunities for grabbing the headlines. Stan
Bonky MP should be warned, though. It may be deeply satisfying to watch yourself, filled with righteous indignation on
the evening news, and go to bed quietly confident that, come
the morning, your picture will be on the front of everything
from the *Financial Times* to the *Daily Star*; but back at the
House of Commons you will be known for precisely what you
are, a self-aggrandising dickhead.

Jim Sillars, previously MP for Glasgow Govan, had developed
this particular technique to a fine art. A good example of classic Sillars spoiling was his performance on 14 March 1989. The
Labour Leader, Neil Kinnock, was called to speak to a Private
Notice Question, which he intended to use to have a go at the
Chancellor, Nigel Lawson. A reasonable and worthwhile
undertaking for any Opposition Leader, you might have
thought. Jim was having none of it, despite being nominally as
opposed to the Conservative Chancellor as was Mr Kinnock
himself.

Neil Kinnock had barely got to his feet, and certainly not
opened his mouth, before Jim was in with his first point of
order. The Speaker told him that he would take points of
order after the Private Notice Question was through, and suggested that until then Jim should sit down and shut up. Advice
he did not take. Neil Kinnock managed to get a mere ten
words out in the next ten minutes or so, as he was ceaselessly
interrupted by Jim Sillars, trying to put the point of order
which he had already been told he could not put.

The whole scene assumed a surreal edge, with Jim Sillars and
Neil Kinnock looking not unlike the weathermen: as one got
up the other sat down, and as one sat down the other stood up.
Finally, after telling Mr Sillars for the *twelfth* time to shut up,
the Speaker did the decent thing, and chucked him out. What
was the point of it all? You may well ask. Did he deliberately
seek to get himself thrown out? Perish the thought. Whatever

the motive, it certainly took the shine off Neil Kinnock's speech.

The Budget has always attracted its fair share of such behaviour. The 1988 Budget saw the House suspended for ten minutes, after total uproar greeted Nigel Lawson's announcement that he intended to cut the top rate of income tax to 40%, the continuation of his speech being drowned out by roars of 'Shame! Shame!' from the Labour benches. Just prior to this, however, Alex Salmond of the Scottish Nationalist Party had indulged in a classic piece of attention-grabbing spoiling.

Overcome with emotion at Nigel Lawson's reduction of companies' corporation tax, Alex was quite unable to contain himself. He leapt to his feet to interrupt the Chancellor, crying, 'This is an obscenity.' The Deputy Speaker, Harold Walker, was taking no prisoners, and the overcharged MP was flung out with no more ado. Stan Bonky MP should listen carefully to what MPs had to say immediately afterwards.

The Conservative Patrick Cormack asked the Deputy Speaker to take measures to prevent the 'important proceedings of the House (being) interrupted in order to gain notoriety for idiots'. Brian Wilson, Labour MP for Cunninghame North, gave Mr Salmond an even worse review, asking, 'Is it in order to point out that the cretinous performance that we have just witnessed owed everything to self-publicity and nothing to social concern?'

A similar piece of working-class heroism was perpetuated by Dave Nellist, who in 1988 interrupted Social Security Minister John Moore a mere sixteen times before he was finally ejected, leaving with the defiant cry, 'I shall be back!' Unfortunately, the estimable Coventry MP (and former DJ and club pianist) was not gifted with the power of prophecy, as he subsequently lost his seat in the 1992 General Election, after being deselected by the Labour Party.

Nuts

No one, surely, will ever forget Ron Brown, the former MP for Edinburgh Leith. Cast your mind back to the allegations that he was caught in the House of Commons shower with his 'researcher' Nonna Longden; swiftly followed up by the court case where he was charged with going round to her flat and stealing her knickers. Ron brought his colourful lifestyle into the Chamber. However, his attempt at mace-waving went badly wrong when the mace turned out to be heavier than it looked, and he dropped it, resulting in a large bill for damages. Naturally this got him into considerable trouble with the Speaker and the whips. It was followed up by a so-called 'apology' for his behaviour, which was a classic of the genre.

Ron was down but not out. He climbed back into the ring with an apology for his apology of an apology. Batting on his side was his pair, Tory Sir Nicholas Bonsor, who pleaded with the Speaker for lenient treatment of Ron Brown. 'I ask honourable Members not to use a sledgehammer to crack . . .' The rest of his words were lost in a roar of laughter. Mr Brown was subsequently suspended from the House and had the Labour whip withdrawn. None of this particularly endeared him to his constituency, and only Ron seemed surprised when he was deselected. Perhaps if the House and the Labour Party had been a little more caring, and a little less ready to stick the boot in, Ron might have been better protected from himself.

The Regressive Gene

Occasionally a sort of mass hysteria seems to break out in the Chamber, and Members start to behave as though they're at their first teenage party and they've just drunk too much cheap cider.

One of the many peculiar conventions of the House is that to make a point of order during a division, you have to be wearing a hat. This ludicrous custom is supposedly a hangover from the 19th century. To be noticed amongst fellow MPs milling about on their way to vote in the lobby, the idea was to don a top hat, which would make you stand out so that the Speaker could see you. As excuses for dressing up go, it's the sort of explanation which would fail to convince a credulous six-year-old. But there you have it. An opera hat is kept under the Serjeant-at-Arms' Chair near the door of the Chamber for this very purpose. In March 1993, in the middle of a series of divisions on Rating and Valuation, for no apparent reason, the House went collectively barmy. Half the Labour MPs present suddenly started making points of order. The opera hat was unable to cover the demands of the occasion, and MPs duly showed the sort of inventive resourcefulness for which we elect them. Knotted hankies were utilised, somebody fetched a flat cap, and one particularly adept individual fashioned an impressive tricorn affair from his order paper.

What Stan Bonky should realise is that, although this may seem to be a very jolly jape at the time, in the cold light of day, or the full glare of the TV cameras, it can all look rather foolish. Constituents can be woefully lacking in humour and understanding, especially when they see the person they elected to represent them jumping up and down with a piece of folded newspaper on his head.

Taking the Piss

Some people are sufficiently self-confident to feel that they needn't bother to take the House of Commons seriously. This is a very big mistake. In 1985, the then Employment Minister, Alan Clark, was given a speech by his civil servants on women's employment rights. He disliked the speech intensely (not surprisingly, as he disliked the whole concept intensely) and had his own views on the subject of women's employment rights, which could best be described as colourful.

Instead of rewriting the speech, he went on to a wine-tasting. He then tottered back to the House and up to the despatch box to give his ministerial speech, which he delivered in a tone so replete with sarcasm and disdain as to make it clear he disagreed with almost every word of it. This all came to a sad end when Clare Short, whose views on women's employment rights could be said to be of a rather different hue, got up and accused the minister (in impeccable parliamentary speak) of being 'incapable', as in 'drunk and . . .', and Mr Clark was soon laughing on the other side of his face.

It is a truth universally acknowledged that the House of Commons takes itself immensely seriously. Anyone taking the piss does so at his own risk.

Rogue MPs Get Bottom Marks – the Whips

The Government and Opposition whips' task is to impose discipline on their respective MPs. The Chief Whip heads the operation, backed up by his Deputy, and four or five henchmen. Their concern is totally straightforward. Their sole interest is voting. They want you to turn up to vote the way you're told to, when you're told to. It's as simple as that.

The importance of the whips can be measured almost directly against the size of the Government majority. The tighter the majority, the more cajoling, bullying and energetic arm-twisting the whips have to do. Following the 1992 General Election, the Conservatives were faced with a very small majority, which is likely to fall still further. If you're working on a majority of twenty or below, it only takes around ten MPs to vote with the Opposition and you've lost. The odds on ten MPs out of some three hundred feeling disgruntled at any one time over any one issue are very high. Here's where the whips come in.

Stories of the whips' persuasive methods are legendary. During the passage of the Maastricht Bill, which took up months of parliamentary time, the Government were frequently in danger of losing votes, and on one occasion actually did, as the number of potential rebels on their own benches rose worryingly high. On one particular night of high drama (in November 1992) when John Major scraped through by three votes, a couple of the more sensitive would-be rebels were seen to be in tears after the whips had words, and one Tory MP was spotted by the cameras being physically frog-marched into the Government lobby by determined ministers. Several Members had been physically threatened and graphic and colourful language had been employed. One MP said it 'was like the battle of the Somme', whilst Teresa Gorman, MP for Billericay, said her interview with the whips had been like 'being gang banged'. Tory rebels duly complained of 'black-mail' and 'arm twisting' and intimidation through the local parties. Conservative Central Office was all sympathy. 'Oh, the poor little darlings,' said one Tory official.

The other ability with which whips are credited is the power to be almost omnipresent. As with George Orwell's Big Brother, they are everywhere and watching you. Christopher Hawkins, formerly the Conservative MP for High Peak, recalls that during the period directly before the unseating of Margaret Thatcher, not even the toilets were safe. Furtive meetings of anti-Thatcher plotters took place in the lavatory corner, and every cubicle door had to be checked, in case one of the whips was in there, quietly taking notes.

Whips' do have a range of persuasive carrots to offer, and a few sticks with which to beat the determined recalcitrant.

The Government whips have things a lot easier than their opposite numbers. They have real jobs to offer. It is clearly much more enticing to be made Minister of State for Agriculture, with a higher salary, a chauffeur-driven Rover and your very own red box, than to be told by the Opposition whips that if you're a very good boy or girl you might just get to become number three on the Opposition front bench agriculture team. This translates as no salary increase, no car, no red box, much more work, and, if you're lucky, a chance to slightly influence Opposition agriculture policy and the odd appearance on telly. Before you get carried away by the glamour, it should be pointed out the telly opportunities you get are the ones that the Shadow Secretary of Agriculture, and the number two, have decided are too unimportant, wearying or plain humiliating to bother with. Such, however, is the drive to succeed in the House of Commons, that this unappetising morsel of a career opportunity still garners an impressive number of takers.

In addition to promotion, the Tory whips have a range of treats to offer such as trips to exotic places and the odd paid consultancy to non-discerning companies. On the Labour side the life of a whip is much more difficult. The PLP is notoriously hard to discipline, stuffed full of martyrs *manqué*, oddballs of various hues and the downright stroppy. Such people are not easy to bribe.

The alternative, naturally enough, is that if the caress of the velvet glove fails to excite, take it off and hit them straight in the face with the iron fist.

In terms of threats and punishments, the whips tend to rely on style over substance. They can threaten you with the sack – and a large number of people do lose their front bench positions due to voting against the party line. The difficulty is that, like death, this can only happen once. When you lose your job, and go back to the lowly back benches, what then? They obviously can't sack you twice. There are a number of people who have twigged this wheeze, and made a positive career out of annoying the whips as far as humanly possible. In parliamentary terms, this is known as becoming a 'maverick'. The rest of the world will recognise it as being 'a pain in the arse'.

Aside from sackings and demotions, the whips tend to rely on the time-honoured tactics of out and out bullying. This sounds very crude, but can be surprisingly successful, as the Maastricht votes suggest. It may not seem like it, but MPs are, after all, only human, and will frequently respond quite well to being browbeaten, threatened and intimidated. A favourite whips' trick is to threaten to tell the constituency about the would-be rebellious MP's irresponsible behaviour. The thought of an angry constituency party is enough to make most MPs break out into a cold sweat, and immediate compliance usually results. Whips can also promise to ease over any little difficulties the MP might have got into, either personal or financial. On the converse side, if you are really bloody minded, they can equally promise to give the details of these same little difficulties to the local and national press.

Unless you are extremely robust in physical and psychological health, have led a blameless past life, and are so sure of your principles that you make Joan of Arc look like a ditherer, then it's usually best to do as you're told. The party is, after all, the reason you got elected. No matter how personally wonderful you might be, people voted not for you individually, but rather for the colour of the rosette you wore. Hence the number of pigs' bladders on sticks elected to Parliament. Your stand on Europe, electoral reform or healthy eating no doubt stems from the purest and highest of personal beliefs, but it is of marginally less interest to the general public than the bingo in yesterday's *Sun*. Before making the grand rebellious gesture, it is as well to bear such things in mind.

The Political Rebel's Guide to Survival

Timing

If you're going to do it, do it quickly. Everyone is expected to be difficult when they're young, and MPs are considered young for their entire first parliamentary term. Even if they were first elected on their sixty-third birthday. Youthful follies are forgivable. Remember Neil Kinnock, when a Shadow Minister, refusing his invitation to Charles and Di's Wedding? A decision which may now look perceptive, although such behaviour was never tolerated by Neil when he became Party Leader. In fact, a bit of teenage insubordination is quite a good career move, along the lines of there being more rejoicing over one black sheep returned to the fold, etc etc. However, Stan Bonky should remember that, just as there are few sadder sights than the middle-aged man who continues going to nightclubs in the mistaken belief that no one will notice the join in his toupee, so the MP who fails to move on from those first heady months of adolescent outrage can find that being stuck in a time warp is less fun than watching *Dr Who* might suggest it to be.

High Moral Tone

You need something to rebel about. Both major parties (the smaller ones can't afford the luxury) have well-known figures who make a profession out of being contrary. Here you have to be careful; it could just get you marked down as a semi-unhinged publicity seeker. So what you have to do is find a cause, nail your principles to the public mast and sit there looking ineffably smug and awaiting your longed-for martyrdom, much in the manner of a medieval saint. Your more cynical colleagues will clock this pose for the sort of pious nonsense it really is, but it tends to go down very well with almost everyone else. You will have endless media invitations to go on TV and explain the depths of angst contained in your suffering soul. You will be able to maunder on about 'gut feelings' and 'conscience' to your heart's content, all while looking nobly into the middle distance. It is often called 'doing a Peter Bottomley', after the current MP for Eltham.

Money in the Bank

Bank up your credit. If you are going at some future time to annoy the whips, get ahead whilst the going's good, so the rope round your neck has plenty of slack on it. The job of the whips' office is tiring, tedious and often infuriating. There are endless ways to ingratiate yourself. Turning up on a Friday to make up the numbers when everyone else has gone home; doing a bit of minor leg work; making a speech on fish quotas to keep the debate going when the whips need it. It's not hard to be nice to the whips, and, seeing that so very few people are, they tend to be very appreciative of any little kindness.

One of the Lads

Being a good bloke. (This is rather difficult for women MPs, but with the right approach, it can be managed.) Because of the inordinate amount of time they have to spend in the House of Commons, hanging around the Chamber, the whips tend to have a fondness for anyone who can ameliorate their crucifyingly dull existence. Hence buying the odd drink, bringing them back some duty-free from the trip they let you go on, or coming up with a good bit of gossip, a new joke or anecdote, stands you in very good stead. A bit of affability never hurt anyone.

Lie Like a Trooper

If you're going to lie, at least do it well. Whips, rather like headteachers and policemen, have heard every excuse in the book. If you intend to duck out of a seven o'clock vote to be at the replay of the FA Cup Final you have to bear in mind that the whips are perfectly well aware that you are the MP for Birmingham Safe Seat, and lo! Birmingham City kick off against Arsenal at 7 pm sharp. What's more, they will have had to deal with a sorry crew of Birmingham – and Arsenal – supporting MPs all day, who will have been trailing into the office with tales of their little daughter's birthday party ('She's only five, and she made me promise I'd be there – you wouldn't ask me to let her down would you?), their granny's funeral ('We're a very close family – she's being buried at night according to Armenian custom – I didn't tell you that I was a quarter Armenian before, did I?') or the immensely important invitation that is really for the Good of the Party, ('Personally I'd rather stay and vote, but the man's insisted on meeting me for dinner. He's worth millions and talking about a substantial donation, so I thought I ought to go. Be a pity to let him slip through our fingers'). So it's very hard to put one over on the whips. The very least you can do is to keep track of how often your granny has died and how old your little daughter is supposed to be. In the long run, it's probably best to accept the inevitable, and turn up at Wembley at half time.

Chapter Five

How to Get on TV

It should be taught as part of the political catechism. You Cannot Over Emphasise the Importance of TV. To politicians, and political parties, it is the stuff of life itself. When Margaret Thatcher talked of 'the oxygen of publicity', she knew what she was on about. Basically, the media serves two purposes. The first is worthy and self-evident. Presumably the MP has chosen a political career because he or she has something to say which they believe needs saying, opinions they want to share, a 'message' they want to put across. And a politican is heard by more people during one twenty-second slot on the Nine o'Clock News than could be reached by spending every night of the next ten years addressing public meetings across the country. We live in an age of mass communication, and the politician who doesn't realise and take advantage of this is not doing the job adequately.

Unfortunately, it also has to be acknowledged that there are other forces which drive MPs into the media spotlight, as politics, like other branches of showbiz, has its fair share of self-aggrandising ego maniacs. There are politicians who would trample over a pile of mangled corpses to get into a TV studio, and it is no coincidence that a number have quit Westminster for the better paid job of full-time media personality. Messrs Kilroy Silk, Walden and Parris come most readily to mind. However, Stan should be warned: there are few things that political colleagues hate and despise more thoroughly than the fellow MP who is constantly on the box. That such feelings are almost entirely motivated by jealousy is irrelevant.

The relationship between journalists and MPs reflects that of an old married couple. They need each other, they seem always to have been together, but that doesn't mean they have to like each other. Most MPs despise journalists and vice versa. Each profession distrusts the other hugely and with good cause. There are few MPs who are without a story to tell of how some journo tried to set them up, misquoted or distorted what they said, or simply lied. Similarly there are few journalists who will not be able to regale you with tales of pompous politicians demanding appearance cash, refusing to answer agreed questions or turning up at the wrong studio at the wrong time on the wrong day. On the plus side, the two parties understand the game perfectly. Each side is out to shaft the other. Both know it, and both will do their damnedest to get away with it. This probably explains why the public rate MPs only slightly higher than journalists and cockroaches in the great chain of being.

The MP just arrived at Westminster has a name to make, and an awful lot to learn about the media and its secrets. Unsurprisingly, journalists are not much interested in Stan Bonky, the newly elected MP for Birmingham Safe Seat. After all, there are six hundred and fifty one MPs in the House of Commons, quite a few of them already pretty famous. A further number will be completely unfamous, but by virtue of holding some obscure Government post, will be contacted when something happens in the area for which they are responsible. Hence the general public will probably be blissfully unaware of the current number two in the Department of National Heritage, but if British football fans stage another Euro-riot this currently faceless being, with his special responsibility for sport, will undoubtedly get on TV. Finally, there are the known trouble makers from both major parties, who can be relied upon to say the nastiest things possible about their own party leaders to any journalist willing to listen. Internal dissension makes for good copy, and independent-minded free-thinkers like Ken Livingstone and Nicholas Winterton are always in high demand. With such a galaxy of proven talent to choose from, small wonder that the average journo has scant interest in poor Stan Bonky. What Stan has to do is remember that self-promotion is an art form – he has to *make* himself interesting. There are several ways of making a political name. Some involve high risk strategy, whilst others rely on a couple of years of solid hard work. If you are willing to invest time and effort, a possibility that definitely falls into the 'solid hard work' category is that of becoming a specialist campaigner.

The specialist campaigner *par excellence* is probably Chris Mullin, the Sunderland MP whose work on behalf of the Birmingham Six eventually played a pivotal part in their pardon and release.

This means that Chris now has the 'miscarriage of justice' market rather neatly sewn up, and whenever it turns out that the police have stitched someone up, the judges have imprisoned the wrong person, or the establishment has generally cocked up in a major way, you can bet next month's wages Chris will be on *Newsnight*. Not surprisingly, he's on pretty regularly these days. What has to be borne in mind, however, is that the 'no pain – no gain' factor is a major player here. Chris Mullin's position was secured not only as a result of years of hard and detailed work, but also because he was a single standard bearer, not through choice, but by necessity. It is hard to recall, after the bandwagon euphoria of the release of the Birmingham Six, the Guildford Four and others, that for the vast majority of the period of Chris's campaign, almost the entire world thought the men were guilty. If you have the sort of latter-day saint's personality which will allow you to stand up for the truth when everyone around you thinks you're a dangerous lunatic, if you can keep your head when all about you are losing theirs, and blaming it on you, if you can meet with Triumph and Disaster – you know how it goes – well if you can do all this, then the campaigner's road is the one for you, my son.

If, however, the idea of being called an accomplice to the bloodiest mass murder in history on the front page of the *Sun* unnerves you, perhaps you should think again. It is, of course, possible to become a specialist campaigner for something a little less high-risk, but bear in mind that campaigning for Sunday shopping does not make gripping TV.

A different approach in the search for media fame is to develop a personality. MPs aren't big on personality, and any Member who actually has one will find himself in considerable demand. There are those like Denis Healey and Norman Tebbit, who have something to say, and are given a great deal of air space in which to say it, because they are known to be witty, amusing and interesting.

Stan Bonky should bear in mind that for an MP, personality is very much a double edged sword. Edwina Currie, for example, when junior Health Minister, was much more famous than her boss, Kenneth Clarke. Unfortunately, the cultivation of the blunt, plain-speaking populism which had served her so well was also her downfall. Her remark about salmonella and British eggs made great copy for the journalists, but cost the Government, of which she was a member, a fortune in compensation to farmers. Edwina is never short of newspaper coverage; what she is short of is a job in Government, although to her credit she turned down the post offered by John Major following the '92 Election, allegedly because she didn't want to work with the same Kenneth Clarke, this time in the Home Office.

Perhaps a safer path altogether is that of simply being telegenic, looking like Robert Kilroy Silk – The Bronzed One. You may be a bit dim, and about as exciting as cold porridge, but you look lovely. There are some faces the camera absolutely adores, there are others which look better on radio.

Good-looking politicians have a head start. David Owen, when an MP, was pompous and widely disliked, but got away with both by virtue of being attractive. It is not provable, but probable, that a good half of the well-meaning middle class women who joined the SDP in the early '80s did so, not out of a life-long commitment to social democracy, but mainly because they fantasised about getting into David's trousers. Similarly, Michael Heseltine's electric effect on local Conservative Associations around the country is much to do with blond hair, thrusting machismo and a good tailor. Harriet Harman has held the advantage for a number of years of being the best-looking woman in Parliament, a title for which Virginia Bottomley is no mean contender. When, before the '92 Election, they were both number two in their respective health teams, it was a producer's dream. Forget *Baywatch*, it's Hattie and Ginny on the Six o'clock News, and they're talking about waiting lists!

Some politicians, on the other hand, are beyond salvation in the looks department. No matter what you do with him (black leather, Calvin Klein underwear, Gap jeans), John Selwyn Gummer will never be sexy.

In the world of television, as with the rest of life, luck plays a significant part. An MP should take a close look at the constituency. Airports, prisons and hospitals all offer possibilities. All you need is a hijack, a roof-top protest or a consultant's strike and the arc lights are on you. TV crews from every corner of Europe will beat a path to your door, and as the local MP you will have unlimited access to the airwaves. This sort of thing should be regarded in much the same light as the understudy getting a chance to go on when Kenneth Branagh goes down with 'flu. You know your lines, it's the chance you've been waiting for, go out there and knock 'em dead!

Whatever happens in a case like this, the fame will probably be short-lived. The hijackers will give up, the prisoners will clamber down from the roof, and the consultants go back to work. Kenneth will recover and play Hamlet once again whilst you wait in the wings. The point is, however, that a lot of people will have seen your performance. If you were good they'll remember, and whilst you won't necessarily get an immediate offer of another starring role, there's every possibility that you might move up from being first spear-carrier to a decent sporting part. There are MPs for whom none of this is possible. Too thick, unpopular and unattractive for any of the options described earlier in this chapter, they take the last alternative – the time-honoured option for the politician who is 'differently skilled'.

This is known in lay parlance as 'becoming a famous lunatic'. There are a couple of well-known practitioners in the present House of Commons, and the trick is really very simple. All you need to do is to concentrate very hard on sex, and what you deem to be sexual perversion. Hence you will lose no opportunity to talk about 'unnatural sex'. You will paint a dark and fantastic picture of the nation's youth, corrupted by teachers, scoutmasters, vicars and anyone else you can think of. The said corrupters of our youth ought to be castrated, flogged, strung up, roasted over a slow fire, hanged at Tyburn, and so on. If you can contrive to bring an element of witchcraft into this, so much the better.

You will also have a great deal to say about unmarried mothers, teenage pregnancy, wife swapping, sodomy in the armed forces and swearing on TV. What you do is to think yourself into the frame of mind appropriate to a deranged 16th-century religious bigot, whose wife has refused to have sex with him for the past two years. Once you've got into this, there will be no stopping you. The downside, of course, is that you'll be obliged to make a complete and utter tit of yourself on a permanent basis. But the point is that you'll often be doing so on prime time TV.

Television in the Chamber

It is probably fair to say that in terms of cultural and behavioural change one of the most world-shattering events on the British political scene was the introduction of television cameras into the Chamber of the House of Commons in November 1990.

The televising of events in the House had been under discussion for a number of years. Arguments raged, and the pro and anti groups expressed themselves in the usual frank and uninhibited fashion.

Peter Shore MP observed that there had been a hoo-hah when

journalists were finally permitted to take notes in 1803, and another to-do when the radio mikes were admitted to the Chamber in 1978. However, no matter how antediluvian the cause, few MPs will pass up the chance for a barney.

Maureen Hicks, the ex-Wolverhampton Tory MP, felt that the 'wildcat behaviour' in the Chamber would have a poor effect on the nation's youth. Her Tory colleague, Sir John 'Bull' Stokes, was worried about the showing of Prime Minister's Question Time interrupting viewers' 'high tea'. 'Are we not supposed to be the gentlemen of England?' he cried to fellow MPs, 'and are the gentlemen of England going to allow this vulgarity?'

Labour MP Joe Ashton (Bassetlaw), who's never been averse to a good dollop of publicity himself, felt that as television had killed off football and religion, the House of Commons would admit the dreaded cameras at its own peril. Geoffrey Dickens MP and Andrew Faulds MP, both remarkable figures in their own right, fought a selfless battle against the intrusion of the cameras – selfless because they were both aware that stardom awaited. 'People have been kind to me,' Mr Dickens explained. 'They've said "Geoffrey, it's made for you. Get in there".' Or as Mr Faulds pointed out, 'It's all very well for the interesting and arresting and knowledgeable extroverts such as myself . . . but what about the others?'

Despite such heroic self-sacrifice, the march of progress was not to be denied, and the cameras duly arrived. As with many great changes, it all seemed jolly shocking at first. The lights were too hot and too bright, and some MPs took ostentatiously to wearing dark glasses, so that the Chamber resembled a Mafia convention. MPs were also understandably dismayed to find that as the TV shot concentrated on the head of the Member speaking, the picture on screen was of someone talking, surrounded by disembodied crotches of seated colleagues. Dark mutterings were heard about certain individuals hogging the limelight. Really, though, these were just teething problems. Everything soon settled down, and it seemed impossible to remember what life was like without the cameras. The head and shoulders shot was soon replaced by the wide-angled view of the Chamber, and then reaction shots of those listening rather than speaking. No one has seen fit to complain about this clear breach of the ground rules, and no one is likely to. One thing was noticeable, though. MPs had changed, changed utterly, and although it might be stretching things to say 'a terrible beauty was born,' there was certainly an attention to personal appearance that may hitherto have been lacking.

In the 1980s and before, a Labour MP seeing a man with a red tie in the vicinity of the House could greet said person with a cheery 'Good morning, Brother!' Red was the colour of the flag, and the wearer was quite obviously a comrade. Unfortunately, such simple verities no longer hold. As any image consultant will tell you, red is a very good colour for television – it makes you stand out. Nowadays the man with the red tie could be a Tory Social Security Minister, not really anybody's idea of a comrade.

If the TV cameras encouraged a flourishing of bright ties and rather smarter suits amongst male MPs, they allowed the women to gain sweet revenge. The House of Commons is a very male club. Of the current six hundred and fifty one MPs, only around sixty are women, a small improvement on previous parliaments, but still pitiably few. Trying to juggle children with the demands of a political career is not easy, and women are denied the priceless back-up of a parliamentary wife, something many of their male colleagues have access to, and not always their own. An endless supply of clean clothes and hot meals, a tidy home and a faultlessly organised personal life are not something to be sniffed at, especially when you're staggering back utterly exhausted after a 1 am vote for the third night running. Women (with the exception of the Finchley bag lady) have had a rather thin time of it in the House of Commons, but TV has been their salvation.

After the eyesight blurs at the rows upon rows of sober dark suits, it is a positive relief to see Margaret Beckett in damask pink, Teresa Gorman in saffron yellow, Hilary Armstrong in emerald green or Gillian Shepherd in unashamed scarlet.

When the cameras came in, the women saw their opportunity and went for it. Although outnumbered by men to the tune of nine to one, their presence in the Chamber is far more noticeable, and the elegance of the turnouts little short of astounding.

If the cameras have smartened up MPs' dress, than they have also had a noticeable effect on behaviour, and despite the dire warnings, the introduction of the camera has not led to daily demonstrations and regular expulsions.

Mace-waving, for example, previously such a favoured recourse of the over-excited elected representative, is now desperately out of fashion, possibly because even the MP who is quite overwhelmed with fury has at the back of his mind the thought that brandishing a very heavy piece of ceremonial gilt is going to make him look a right prat on telly. The practice beloved by front bench members down the ages, of putting their feet up on the table in front of the Speaker's chair, has also gone. The political great and good took one look at the pictures, noted the startling resemblance between themselves in this posture and lounging schoolboys with their feet on the desk, and there was an end to it. Front bench feet, at least in the literal sense, are now firmly on the ground.

The advent of the cameras has also meant that there are rather fewer sightings of the now almost extinct *Member electus – tired et emotionalis*. In kinder times, when the world was young, you could catch sight of all manner of MPs staggering to their feet after a 'good dinner' to proclaim their opinions on the evils of the modern world. That the thought process was often extremely hard to follow, and the word enunciation such as to give the Hansard record takers a nightmare, in no way detracted from the bravura nature of the general performance. In the good old days it wasn't only superannuated backbenchers with nothing to lose who indulged in this specialised form of communication. Even the very great, such as Foreign Secretaries, were known to have a go. Indeed, the very phrase 'tired and emotional' was invented to describe one of George Brown's more colourful political moments. Things are now

very different; one can no more imagine Douglas Hurd standing at the despatch box totally pissed, and maundering on
about 'bloody foreigners' until he fell over, than you can
visualise the Queen taking up lambada. TV has had a very
sobering effect. No more can you contemplate, as happened in
the 1960s, a senior member of the Government, after one glass
of port too many, leaning over to the ambassador's wife at a
foreign embassy dinner to ask, 'Do you fuck?' Understandably shocked, the women replied,'Minister, you must get
your face slapped very often.' 'Yes,' he replied happily, 'but I
also get an awful lot of fucks.' This sort of repartee really isn't
Douglas Hurd's style.

This is not to say, however, that the game is entirely up. There
are still a couple of brave souls who are completely undaunted
at the thought of their electorate glued to their armchairs saying to each other, 'Look at him, Jean, he's pissed!' 'You're
right, Jeremy, he's fallen over. No, no, he's up again. You
can't understand a word he's saying though.' Dinosaurs from
another age they may be, but you have to admire the almost
noble disregard they have for the good opinion of the world at
large. They are not to be cowed by the modern world of mass
communication. They have always gone through life drinking
far too much and then getting up and talking utter rubbish,
and damned if they're going to stop now.

Tricks of the Trade

Getting on TV is both an art and a craft. The craft element,
like any other set of skills, is merely a trade which has to be
learned.

The basic building block of personal publicity is the press release. Journalists, despite what they might tell you, are not
endowed with powers of second sight. Unless you tell them
what you are up to, they are not going to know, except if you
don't actually want them to know what you're getting up to,
then they're bound to find out. Hence whenever Stan Bonky
MP does anything even faintly interesting, he should ensure a

press release is sent out to the requisite people. Just who these people are will depend on what he is doing.

MPs, as part of their job, do lots of things in the constituency which are of no interest to the national media whatsoever. Joining the protest and signing the petition against the building of a new by-pass though Morton Stanley is of negligible concern either to the *Financial Times* or *World in Action*. It is, of course, riveting to the residents of Morton Stanley, and a press release should be despatched forthwith to the *Morton Star*, the *Morton and Inchley Gazette* (freesheet), *Independent Radio Mortonshire*, *BBC Radio Morton* and, if more than ten people are likely to turn up, to the local BBC and independent TV stations. An MP will soon get to know the local journos on the patch, and should cultivate them. The relationship is symbiotic, both needing the other. The MP, with a view to the next elections, will want to keep a local media profile, and will also recognise the usefulness of the local press in influencing local decisions. The Morton-based media will long ago have accepted the fact that toss all of any interest actually happens in Morton, and will regard the MP as a sort of cash cow, who can always be relied upon to fill up some of the acres of empty space on their programme or paper. Hence there is a cosy sense of shared purpose which the intelligent MP will do well to foster. No mater how famous you get, it always pays to make time for the local media, as you never know when you will need them. Chris Patten, now tucking into chicken chow mein in Hong Kong, is an interesting example of a man who got too big for his constituency. He lost his seat in Bath not, regrettably, because of the lies he told about the Labour Party in the 1992 General Election, but because his duties as Tory Party front man made it impossible for him to fight the sort of campaign necessary for such a highly marginal constituency.

The national media is a different and more difficult game. They will only respond to a press release if it suggests that you are up to something of world-shattering importance, and sometimes not even then. Likewise you should only call a press conference if you have something to produce which will persuade the hacks to turn up. Leaked documents are an absolute winner, but quite hard to come by, and for policy documents you need to be on the front bench. It is often helpful to get a supporting cast to accompany you; children, animals and people in fancy dress are almost guaranteed to get the cameras out. Hence if you are interested in animal welfare and want to protest about fur farms and trapping, a small army of tots dressed up in the cuddliest Arctic fox and baby seal costumes available is a sound bet. If that doesn't get you the ITN news and a 'picture story' in the *Independent*, nothing else will. But don't overdo it, because the journos might be more interested in the side-show than in you, and that will never do.

The other thing with which the aspiring MP will have to come to terms is the strange body of exotic creatures collectively known as 'the lobby'. The lobby is made up of a small coterie of journalists attached either to the major newspapers or to particular TV and radio stations. They get their name from the special pass they carry, which allows them, alone of all mortals, to stand in Members' Lobby whilst the House is in session, thus giving highly privileged access to MPs as they come and go in and out of the Chamber.

Much like ravens on a battlefield, small knots of lobby correspondents hang around in this hallowed space, waiting for their chosen victim to emerge from the relative safety of the Chamber. Once their prey is spotted, they swoop, and are impossible to dislodge until they have the quote they seek. It is in the nature of the lobby that many of these quotes are unattributable. Tory MPs will whisper confidingly to a lobby journalist that Michael Heseltine's a busted flush, John Major doesn't know what day it is, Lady Thatcher is two sandwiches short of a picnic. This will translate on to the news as 'growing backbench concern over the Government's apparent lack of direction'. Lobby journalists are the modern equivalent of the priests who read the entrails in ancient Greece and Rome. They deal in the language of nods and winks, rumour and counter-rumour. When not hanging around the Members'

Lobby they can usually be found in one of Westminster's many bars.

They are also very useful for free lunches, all on expenses, of course. It is quite amazing how easy it is to gather inside information from MPs for the mere price of a couple of large G and Ts.

So much for the basics. What about when the cameras actually start rolling? The best thing to do is start at the bottom. Donuting is a relatively easy thing to master. The term came to public attention when the cameras first came to the Chamber. Because of the tightness of the shot, a few Members gathered round the minister, and would give the appearance of him addressing a packed and attentive House. Little did the viewer know that beyond this small band of enthusiasts were rolling acres of empty green benches, resembling the fields of Kent rather than the House of Commons. With the advent of the longshot, which revealed the appalling truth, donuting has died, thus leaving our parliamentary orator often looking lost and slightly forlorn. However, there are still occasions when it really pays dividends to be part of a political audience in the Chamber: if you are an MP from Scotland or Wales, when you know that Scottish or Welsh Questions will be covered extensively on local TV. Being seen in the Chamber, even if not asking a Question, puts you quids in. Given the extraordinary coverage of Prime Minister's Questions, if you can get within camera shot of the Member asking a Question, you stand a good chance of getting on every news programme. Your mother and your constituents will love it.

To do this really professionally you should also be able to summon up a number of convincing expressions, covering interest, thoughtfulness, disgust, admiration and righteous indignation. You should also be able to say 'Hear hear!', 'Oh yes', 'It's true' and 'Rubbish!' when required. Gestures such as accusatory pointing, strongly affirmative head nodding (Ann Widdecombe, Conservative MP for Maidstone, is a spectacular nodder – you would be proud to have her on the back shelf of your car), contemptuous head shaking and loud, forced laughter are well worth cultivating.

Once you have got this sorted, you can break out on your own, and polish up some more individual skills. In the last decade the term 'soundbiting' has come into prominence. As news bulletins have got shorter and snappier the demand has increased for the memorable phrase, which will sum up a complicated argument, and fit nicely into a sixty-second news item. Hence the soundbite.

Soundbites should be about three to ten seconds long, self-explanatory, easily used out of context and designed to stick in the mind. Alliteration is important here – 'more mortgage misery' is easier to remember than 'a lot of mortgage unhappiness'. Likewise, using slang is often better than going for grammatical purity: Macmillan's 'You've never had it so good', or Thatcher's 'U turn if you want to' and Reagan's 'This one's for the gippa'. The last is total gibberish to anyone born this side of the Atlantic, but seemed to go down terribly well in America. Rewriting well-known saws and sayings is a useful technique, well employed by David Mellor: for example, his election quote 'Dogs bark, cats miaow and Labour raise taxes', or the famous, and with hindsight definitely ironic, remark that the press were 'drinking in the Last Chance Saloon'. Few people have the ability to toss these remarks about at will, and the keen would-be media star would be well advised to sit down and put a great deal of thought and effort into incorporating such spontaneous phrases into future speeches or articles. But again, Stan should beware. If you practise too hard you may lose the ability to speak normally or communicate in anything other than soundbites, which can be very unsettling at dinner parties (this crunchy chicken's crackin'!) or in your family life (pesky kids pile on the pressure). A sad and tragic case of the soundbite biting back is Gordon Brown MP, whose love of the device for a time seriously threatened his political career, as people forgot that he was actually capable of completing a sentence. Whatever you do, don't overdo it.

Another useful political tool, for very different circumstances, is grandstanding. Grandstanding is shorthand for 'playing to the grandstand'. What it means is working yourself up to a lather of passion, indignation and excitement, in the sure knowledge that the cameras are recording every minute of it. Properly employed, this technique will get you a reputation for being a great orator and also someone who genuinely cares. A classic example of this was given by one of Labour's defence spokesmen, John Reid, speaking in the 1993 army debate about proposed cutbacks in army personnel. Our brave lads, he said, out there amidst the horrors of war-torn Bosnia, would be 'dying with their redundancy notices in their hands'. Predictably enough, he got excellent TV and radio coverage. It is, however, a technique which should be used with caution. Too frequent or indiscriminate recourse to grandstanding will ensure that you get lumped with the dwindling band of *tired et emotionalis*, which is not what you wanted at all.

Personal presentation is also very important in the TV world. For example, there is the knotty question of ties. Research has been done which shows that if you are doing a long stint on TV, like appearing on *Walden*, or doing an interview with one of the many Dimblebys, you should wear a bright and snazzy tie. The reasoning behind this is that it will make you look colourful and interesting, and the viewer will be impressed by your sharp appearance. But should you be in line for a quickie – thirty seconds on the Six o'clock or Nine o'clock News – your tie should be sober and discreet. If you ignore this rule, the people watching will apparently spend your entire appearance time discussing whether they like your tie or not, without listening to a single word you've said. This of course holds true for women in terms of earrings, brooches and the colour, pattern and style of whatever they wear above the waist.

The most vexed and panic-inducing area in the whole gamut of personal appearance problems, is, of course, hair. Men have a real problem. TV (as Bryan Gould has discovered) has an un-canny knack of revealing previously well-hidden bald or thinning spots, not only revealing, but sometimes seeming positively to dwell on, the offending area which, to make matters worse, shines like a beacon under the studio lights. Baldness on a MP need not be a handicap, as long as you are willing to face the inevitable. Side partings a centimetre above your right ear, forward combing and, worst of all, toupees, are to be avoided at all costs; although it must be said that since the advent of the TV cameras the number of MPs sporting dead gerbils on their heads seems to have increased. Recent Labour Leaders have been highly successful at dealing with the political problem of being follicularly challenged, both Neil Kinnock and John Smith going for the short, neatly combed and dignified approach – which has had the effect of making their hair a non issue.

Messy hair is a perennial nightmare for politicians, and it is a fact that there has never been a British Prime Minister with flyaway, problem hair. The public seem to associate the inability to control your hair with the inability to control yourself, and an out-of-control politician is not an attractive thought. Blonde *übermensch* looks are big in the Conservative Party, and a whole host of Thatcher lookalikes now populate the Conservative benches, all of whom have big blonde hair. The prize for unashamed blonde-from-a-bottle should probably be divided between Michael Fabricant MP and Marion Roe MP, although Marion Roe ought to win on a split (ends) decision as she has at least enough blonde hair to spare for another couple of Thatcher-clone MPs without noticing the difference. Since his election in 1992, speculation in the House of Commons has been rife as to whether Mr Fabricant's hair is real. Surely it must be, since nobody as rich as Mr Fabricant would have purchased such a preposterous wig. Whatever the truth, he is still called 'Worzel Gummidge' by friend and foe alike.

Gordon Brown is gifted with probably the nicest hair in the House of Commons, thick, luxuriant, midnight black with a slight wave. The effect is slightly spoilt by the fact that most weeks he forgets to wash it. The Edinburgh MP, Alistair Darling, has an interesting combination of silver hair and a

black beard, which either makes him look sexy and distinguished, or like a *Star Trek* extra, depending on your taste.
John Patten's hair has a life and personality of its own, which
seeing that its owner has not much in the way of either, is
probably a good thing.

On the down side, male MPs are notoriously prone to dandruff, and frequently appear on television with what appears
to be a small snowstorm settling on their suit jackets. Fortunately, clothes' brushes have been thoughtfully provided in all
MPs' cloakrooms, and Stan would be well advised to make use
of them, along with a standard anti-dandruff shampoo. The
other thing the neophyte Member should strongly resist is the
awful temptation to give in to facial hair. Few apart from Alistair Darling get away with them. Beards are all very well for
sociology lecturers and old thespians, such as Andrew Faulds,
MP for Warley East, but are not a good idea otherwise. While
we're on personal appearance: false teeth – for God's sake
make sure they fit properly. There are few things more embarrassing than losing your dentures half-way through a speech,
as former Tory MP, Sir Anthony Beaumont Dark, can testify.
Speaking in a televised debate with particular passion, his
plate suddenly shot out. With the presence of mind that has
undoubtedly gained him a knighthood, Sir Anthony brought
superhuman powers to bear, and pushed the offending falsies
back in his mouth before they fell to the floor. The whole spectacular occurrence, thanks to cameras being in the Chamber,
was replayed on every news programme you'd care to mention.

So having shaved off your Zapata moustache, taken to
washing your hair every other morning, written your press releases, chatted up the lobby correspondents, inveigled your
sister's children into dressing up as small furry animals for the
good of your career, donated, soundbit, grandstanded and
shouted 'Yes!' 'No!' and 'Rubbish!', what else is there left to
learn? Well, there is one final secret, and children, don't try
this one at home.

Spin doctors are the necromancers of political press management. Like wizards of legend, gifted with special powers, they are readers of secret runes and the beneficiaries of long years of patient study. They deal in dangerous and highly flammable material, working in conditions where one slip could prove fatal.

The British spin doctor *par excellence* is Peter Mandelson, the erstwhile TV producer and Labour Party media supremo, and current MP for Hartlepool. What Mr Mandelson perfected was the art of turning a story around. By stressing a particular angle, suggesting a line of inquiry or giving out a juicy quote, he would bend and influence the journalistic perception of a political event to his own advantage. For example, say a group of Labour MPs rebelled against the whip and voted contrary to Neil Kinnock's wishes. The hacks would begin typing up their piece about 'Labour Party Split'. Peter would then explain to them what the *real* story was. Had they noticed how few MPs voted the wrong way? Had they seen that X, the well known left winger, had in fact voted with Neil? Had they heard the rumours that one of the prominent rebels was just about to be voted off the Labour Party's ruling executive, some might say as proof of the party's displeasure at his disloyalty? Wasn't the real story about how firm Neil's grip was on the party as a whole, how rebellions were becoming smaller and more futile? Utterly seduced, the hacks would completely re-write their original draft.

How to Survive the Politicial Interview

If you become successful in your career as a politician, sooner or later you will have to learn to cope with the round of speciality programmes which make up the staple diet of the political media. There is no fail safe approach, and many politicians who have been doing it for years still come horribly unstuck. However, for the keen self-improver, there are a few handy tips which might come in useful.

Election Night Specials

Election night TV can either be several hours of the purest form of torture or a marvellous opportunity to wallow in the suffering of your enemies. This depends entirely on whether your side is winning or losing.

If you are winning you can stick the boot into the other side while they're down, but not with so much relish that you offend the viewing public. In other words, give them a good kicking, but remember to wear your slippers. If your side are losing, cling to key phrases, such as, 'We have a great deal of be encouraged about', or 'In many ways this is a very good result for us', or 'This was never a seat we were looking to do particularly well in'. You will have to keep a sickly smile on your face, and laugh through clenched teeth as your opponents make witty little sallies at your expense. No one likes a bad loser, and no matter how much you might want to punch the lights out of the bastard sitting next to you, restrain yourself, at least till you're off the camera. Of course, *in extremis*, you can always get honest, and admit that your party has been completely stuffed, by virtue of having crap policies and a total shit for a candidate.

Question Time and *Any Questions*

The problem with both of these programmes is that you are dealing with members of the general public, who can be extremely difficult and ungrateful. You will need to be alert to whatever the 'issues of the week' are likely to be and, better still, to have an opinion on them. In fact, so important have these programmes become that all major parties offer their MPs a full briefing before they appear, so there really is no excuse. Try to sound reasonable and intelligent, if at all possible, and no matter how hostile or rude the questioner is, never, but never, retaliate. To do so will always come over as bullying and hectoring. Both these programmes tend to have an off-the-wall question to end with. This is usually along the predictable lines of 'Who would you like to be marooned on a desert island with?', or 'If you could send someone into space, who would it be?' In both cases, depending on whether you are Tory or Labour, the correct answer is 'Mrs Thatcher'.

The Men Who Sit in Judgement

Jeremy Paxman is renowned for extreme rudeness and will kick off by asking you a question of such breathtaking insolence that you will be tempted to make him eat his teeth. Witness his interview with 'Pretty Boy' Portillo, Chief Secretary of the Treasury, after the 1993 Budget: 'Mr Portillo, would you like to take this opportunity to apologise to the British people?' This is the political equivalent to 'Have you stopped beating your wife?' There is no easy way to deal with Paxman. Just keep steady and don't lose your cool, and vow to yourself that you will get him in the green room afterwards. But remember, it was Mr Paxman who famously said that when interviewing a politician, he was always thinking, 'Why is this lying bastard lying to me?' Jeremy Paxman will never get a knighthood.

Brian Walden is a man of one idea. Before you go on he will have identified one answer, one admission he wants to get out of you. The entire programme will be structured to this end. It's up to you to avoid it. This is not actually all that difficult, Walden's questions being so ridiculously long that you have an inordinate amount of time to think of an answer, or indeed to slip out of the studio, unnoticed by Mr Walden.

Jon Snow is a nice man, who comes over as a nice man. His technique is to sound particularly sympathetic and understanding, and just when he's lulled you into thinking what a decent chap he is, he will deliver the knock-out punch. Bear in mind that no matter how decent he seems, he is not your best friend, but a newscaster, who is trying to turn you inside out. Mr Snow is also incredibly tall and wears extremely bright ties.

Jonathan Dimbleby, like most very short men, has a large chip on his shoulder. He's big on homework, and will probably remind you of something you said in 1979, which directly contradicts the line you are currently peddling. It is a good idea to put aside plenty of time for research and preparation before the interview, with a view to being at least as well informed as he is.

Fringe Benefits

When MPs become really well known, they start getting asked to appear on a variety of what could be called 'general interest' programmes. Some of these are good fun, and relatively foolproof. Others should be avoided like the plague. The plague carriers are as follows:

The Psychiatrist's Chair – an absolute killer. Known for the number of guests who burst into tears halfway through. No serious politician is going to tell the truth on this programme. To do so will only make you sound precious beyond belief, and ensure that you become a laughing stock amongst your colleagues.

Youth programmes. The only reason they want you on is to make a fool of you. They will laugh at your clothes, your hair and your views. Your fellow guest will probably be a braindead American rap artist who's in an altered state.

Have I Got News For You. This is a difficult one. It has an enormous audience, but the programme has become a vehicle for the humour of Ian Hislop and Paul Merton, which is frequently directed at visiting politicians. If you are into S&M this is the one for you. Only two politicians have ever really shone on the programme, Neil Kinnock and the Rt Hon. Tub of Lard, who stood in for Roy Hattersley.

Desert Island Discs. This can be okay, but whatever you do, check your selection with a wide and reliable group of friends before going on. No one is going to take you seriously if you confess that you want to take Bananarama or Barry Manilow to your desert island. David Blunkett will be known forever as the man who chose a Nana Mouskouri record. Where were the spin doctors? Somebody should have told him. On the other hand Dennis Skinner was a great success. Truth to tell, the Beast of Bolsover revealed himself as an unreconstructed romantic.

Chapter Six

How to Have a Good Time

Amazingly enough, many members of the public labour under the delusion that being an MP is just one long party. They seem to think that if a Member of Parliament isn't taking Pamella Bordes out to a nightclub, or having various parts of his anatomy sucked by Antonia de Sancha, he must be on a 'fact finding' trip to Bangkok or on a free holiday in Marbella. As Stan Bonky MP can testify, this is sadly not the case. Politics is hard graft and hard work. If you want to have a good time, it doesn't come easy; in fact you have, so to speak, really got to put your back into it.

Receptions

When first elected, Stan Bonky will be surprised and excited by the bewildering number of invitations that arrive through the post. Many of them will be from various lobby and pressure groups, who will want him to attend their annual reception.

Receptions are unpredictable beasts. They can range from the utterly crap – warm white wine and peanuts in a draughty room with the ten most boring people on the planet – to the totally wonderful – champagne and quails' eggs in the Sainsbury Wing of the National Gallery. The trick is to learn how to spot the dross in advance, and this can only come with experience, but a good tip is to seek out the House of Commons' red-nose tendency, and ask one of them to give you a steer.

Basic general rules apply, although they are not infallible. The more money an organisation has, the more likely it is to push the boat out at the reception. Hence a reception thrown by the Keep Duty Free Campaign or the City of London will not disappoint, whilst the do given by the Welsh Arts Council is likely to prove more rudimentary. There, is however, a catch to all this, namely that if Loadsamoney plc, or whoever, have spent an absolute fortune on venue, champagne and delicate niceties for you to nibble, they rather selfishly are going to want something in return. 'Something' translates as your complete attention for about two and a half hours, with probably a speech thrown in.

You will have wandered through the door, got a glass in one hand and a nice little smoked salmon canapé in the other, and be happily heading towards your mates, who you've spotted over the other side of the room, and crash, the whole evening will suddenly start to fall apart. A man in an expensive suit with a lapel badge that says 'Tim Foster – Director of Marketing' will have approached on your blind side, and his hand will be on your shoulder. 'Stan!' he will cry 'Stan Bonky! So pleased you could make it!'

He will then start to talk to you. He will probably say things like, 'So, what can I tell you about our little outfit?' Or, 'How much do you know about what we're doing in marketing terms?' The truthful answer to this is 'Sod all, and I care even less', but of course you can't say that. The really excruciating thing is that whilst he's boring you rigid for what seems like an eternity, grinding on about market penetration among AB1s in the south-east of England, you will, out of the corner of your eye, be able to see your colleagues. They will be consuming vast quantities of champagne, and attacking the ever-dwindling supply of rare delicacies. At this point resist the temptation to smack Tim firmly in the teeth and lunge towards the table. This would not be a wise career move, and you must content yourself with the knowledge that he will, eventually, have to let you go – particularly as his eyes will be flickering perpetually over your left shoulder, on the look-out for his next victim. At last it will be over. He will then say that it has been really fascinating to talk to you, but he must let you move on. Now you can concentrate on what you came to the reception to do – eat and drink. But quick as a flash, and grasping you firmly by the elbow, he will deliver his fatal parting shot. 'Before I leave you I must just introduce you to Trevor; Trevor Dougal, our European distributions man. I know he wants to talk to you about EC cheese quotas.' In this way the inexperienced reception attender will be passed from one ear-bashing to the next. By the end of the two hours you will be wishing you'd become a serial killer rather than an MP.

The newcomer must remember, as the invites roll in, to beware of the reception that looks to be, on paper, absolutely delightful, but can, in certain circumstances, be nothing short of a community service order. The proffered trip down the Thames on the good ship *Freebie* sounds like a fine idea. You can picture it, the evening sun casting long shadows on the rippling water, agreeable music gently playing, and interesting people indulging in bright and witty conversation, as you float past the finest sights in London. There's no need to be totally cynical – this *can* come off – but the odds are not the sort that you would be advised to bet on. More likely it will be chilly, possibly damp as well. The boat will lurch about, caught by the swell of passing craft, and you will begin to feel sick. Worse still, someone else will *be* sick. You will decide that you want to go home, and then the full agony will hit you, YOU CAN'T GET OFF! That's right, you're stuck there, and when you make inquiries, which the seasoned MP will have told Stan he ought to have done before he ever set foot on the gangplank, the organisers will cheerily tell you that the boat's sailing down to Greenwich, turning round, and they hope to dock in another three hours. A point of important advice, no matter how desperate you get – don't jump. It's further than it looks, and the Thames has a very nasty undertow.

The final thing to remember about receptions is to read the invitation. Simple advice, you might think, but easily forgotten. If this rule is followed, a wealth of useful information will be gleaned, which will allow you to judge the evening ahead. Some receptions are smart, some are not. Some are little more than good-natured piss-ups, some serious networking sessions. At some you'll be able to meet people who really know about a field you're interested in, and talk to them in a relaxed fashion. At others you'll be introduced to more Tims, Trevors, Bobs and Fionas than you realised existed in the English-speaking world. If the information on the invite isn't clear about the sort of do it's going to be, either ring up yourself, or get your office to do it. This way you will avoid the calamitous error of John Reid, a Scottish Labour MP, who like so many west-coast Scots, is of Irish extraction.

One autumn evening, following the 7 pm vote, John made his way to the Jubilee Room in the House of Commons, a favoured reception venue. It was the Labour Party Irish Section do, a renowned good time, at which many of his Celtic colleagues were due to turn up. Revving himself up for what he was sure was going to be a great night, he approached the Jubilee Room, and as he got near the door, started singing the well-known, and rousing, Irish Rebel song, *The Boys From The Old Brigade*. 'Where are the lads who stood with me/ When history was made?' he carolled as he burst through the door. Well, not here, was the answer, as he gazed upon an almost silent room, semi-filled with people in dark suits and dresses. Never mind, he thought, I'm early. The other lads will be here soon. In the meantime he was approached by someone who asked if he wanted a drink. A whisky, John said, would be grand. The man looked rather unhappy: We don't have any whisky,' he replied. 'Would you like some tea?' Slightly bemused, John Reid took his cup of tea and surveyed the room. 'It's a bit dead, isn't it?' he asked. His companion winced and said nothing. Undeterred, the MP sailed onwards, 'So when is the music and the drink going to get here?' he inquired. 'This lot look like they've just been to a funeral'. It was at this juncture that his disconcerted host felt compelled to tell John that he was at the reception of the National Bereavement Society. The Irish reception was in fact going on at the same time, but in an entirely different place.

Foreign Trips

Is it a bird? Is it a plane? No, it's Michael Clark MP and the Inter Parliamentary Union. When it comes to high-class foreign trips, the IPU really are the dog's bollocks, as granny used to say. They are closely followed in the am-MP-will-travel stakes by the Commonwealth Parliamentary Association, who are first class in terms of Africa, Australia, India and so on, but unfortunately, by their very nature, a bit of a non-starter when it comes to America, North and South, and indeed almost everyone else that wasn't coloured pink on the 19th-century globe. But one thing is common to both organisations, as Dennis Skinner famously pointed out: they never arrange fact-finding trips to Greenland in the winter.

In their latest (1991) published annual report, the IPU have a section which they rather coyly entitle 'Outward Delegations'. To you or me, this translates as 'Foreign Trips'. Under this section, various MPs who have been on 'outward delegations' published their findings which make interesting reading . . . Among countries visited were: Argentina, (which due to the recent war seems to have been a depressingly work-orientated and dour occasion), Mexico, lots of fun and great sight seeing. Libya (a bit of a disappointment in the social stakes, not surprisingly). Zaire, Saudi Arabia, Yemen, Israel, Jordan, Syria and Turkey – sun, sand, sea and by all accounts excellent nosh. Swiftly followed by Bulgaria (not to be recommended, in fact it all sounds a bit grim) and Albania which, likewise, was no fun at all.

The rival CPA was content with Belize, Canada, Isle of Man (shome mishtake surely), Perth (Australia, dear, not Scotland) and, rather bizarrely, a conference in London. If this list looks a little meagre, it has to be admitted that other regional conferences did take place in Lusaka, Trinidad and Tobago, the Cook Islands and New South Wales (New South Wales, fortunately enough, being very little like old South Wales). There were also a couple of seminars in Sri Lanka and Winnipeg. All in all not a bad effort.

A key piece of advice for Stan Bonky MP, wistfully eyeing the empty pages in his passport, and busy ironing the so far unworn pair of Bermuda shorts he bought on his last trip to Spain, is to remember the two magic words – *all party*. If properly employed they will whisk you round the globe and back again. The incantation is not difficult to learn; look at the weekly notices sent out by the party whips. As well as the depressing stuff about 10 pm votes and campaigning for the local elections, there will be attached pages bearing the headline 'All-Party Notices', 'All-Party', say it slowly, savour the words, and then translate them into air miles.

A casual glance through the all-party notices of 1992 will reveal a plethora of opportunities. The British-Hong Kong Group, the Romania Group, Beginners' German, Spanish Language Class, the Indo-British Parliamentary Group Curry Club Lunch, the IPU Conference in the Cameroon, the British-American Parliamentary Group, the British-Latin American Parliamentary Group, the British-Sudan Group, the British-Danish Group, the British-Venezuelan Group, the Tibet Group, the Arts and Heritage Group (a good one for the discerning traveller), the British-Russian Group, the British-South Pacific Group, the Anglo-Bermudian Group, the CPA Branch Delegation to Mauritius, the Anglo-Tunisian Group, the 89th Inter-Parliamentary Conference in New Delhi, and the fact-finding visit to Denmark. Wonderful, isn't it? The list is endless, and reads like a Thomas Cook guide. The individual who can't be satisfied by the many-faceted gems of the all-party notices really does have difficulty to meet needs.

In fact, for those with a penchant for hair shirts, the all-party notice can also offer succour. For instance, there's the Channel Tunnel Group, or the Joint Meeting of the Scientific Committee/Information Technology Committee on 'supercomputing'. Another attractive option is the Food and Health Forum – 'School Meals – A Case for Reform?' or the equally dashing Parliamentary Roads Study Group. You can't say they don't cater for every taste.

Eking Out the Parliamentary Stipend

Of course, holidays are lots of fun, but at the end of the day, you can't really enjoy yourself without money. Any number of

Ministers have found that life in the fast lane was all very well, but the more you have, the more you want. A ministerial salary, currently around £63,000, might seem like a lot of money. But when you're mixing it with millionaires, and when the majority of your colleagues in the higher echelons of the Tory Party are rich enough to regard £63K as pocket money, your relative poverty becomes irksome.

The time-honoured, and legal, way out of political penury is to take a directorship. In fact, to take several directorships. This is all a bit irritating for ministers, as due to a perceived clash of interests, they're not allowed to do it. The then Arts Minister, Lord Gowrie, resigned for this very reason in 1985, saying that he just couldn't live on his measly ministerial salary. Likewise it is interesting to note the announcement by Patrick Nicholls MP (Hansard 15/6/93). 'Let me begin by declaring my interests in Hill and Smith Holdings, the NSCC Port Enterprises Ltd., the Waterfront Partnership, the Howard de Walden Estates, MinOtels and Dunn and Baker.' Patrick Nicholls had been tipped for a return to junior ministerial office in the Government reshuffle, of summer '93, and had indeed been offered a position, but had turned it down 'for family reasons'. As one political commentator wryly pointed out, the list of directorships in Hansard would have amounted to considerably more than a ministerial salary.

Then there's the case of the former Secretary of State for National Heritage, David Mellor, a man who day after day, night after night, worked flat-out for the arts, until he tragically shot himself in the foot, and in doing so wasted the career of a promising young actress, who just happened to have the said foot in her mouth at the time. Mr Mellor has now gone from being a minister to being a media industry, and it can be quite difficult to find a programme or a paper that he's not on or in. What's a minister's salary compared to the six figures that David Mellor is now reputed to earn? Clearly it does not have to be all up when you get the chop.

But for the impoverished backbencher, none of these tiresome scruples need apply – the field is wide open. The directorships and consultancies are waiting to be garnered. There is, however, a slight stumbling block. For Stan Bonky, Labour MP for Birmingham Safe Seat (urban central), there are difficulties of expectation and form which will never occur for Stanley Brinsley-Bonky, Conservative MP for Birmingham Safe Seat (posh-bit west). Firstly, there are the ethical problems. Stan's constituents will, in large numbers, be on the dole, in low paid jobs, on the verge of being made redundant, or just generally having a bad time of it. They need never know, and will probably never find out, if he takes a directorship, but Stan will know, and when he goes to bed at night, the accusing stares of the poor and the dispossessed will line up to haunt him.

Then there's the rest of the Labour Party. Being, essentially, a deeply moral organisation, the Labour Party doesn't much approve of freeloading and pocket-lining. If they find out, Stan's Constituency Labour Party will give him hell. They will point out, at meeting after meeting, that with his MP's salary of £31,000, he earns roughly four times as much as the average *employed* member of his constituency. Then of course there's the travel allowance, the office allowance, the two homes allowance and so on. Yet apparently this isn't enough for him. How, they will mutter darkly, can he purport to represent working people? Perhaps, they will suggest, with menace, they ought to have an MP who is more in touch with the needs of the area and its inhabitants? If he survives a likely deselection bid, Stan ought to realise that, whilst the Parliamentary Labour Party will just about tolerate greedy bastards, it neither likes nor approves of them. Acquiring a fistful of directorships is not the way to get on in the party, and a quick glance around the current Shadow Cabinet will not yield much in the way of MPs with hefty consultancy fees or whopping fat directorships. The Labour Party admires asceticism and self-restraint, and this extends to matters financial.

Stanley Brinsley-Bonky MP has no such problems with the Tories. A glut of directorships will merely be taken as proof of his financial acumen and good connections. The Conservatives would have applauded Gordon Gekko in the movie *Wall Street*

when he said, 'greed is good'. This party dichotomy is under-
lined in the yearly *Register of Members' Interests*, a House of
Commons document available for public scrutiny, which lists
the outside interests of each Member. Some MPs clearly are in
to moonlighting in a big way.

Bill Cash, MP for Stafford, is 'Adviser to Institute of Legal
Executives, Adviser to Institute of Company Accountants,
Adviser to Council for Complementary and Alternative Medi-
cine, Consultant to Radcliffe's and Co., Adviser to the
National Market Traders' Federation, and Adviser to Politics
International.' David Evans, the cerebral MP for Welwyn and
Hatfield, has a truly impressive array of activities. He has
directorships for Leapsquare Limited, Bradnam Enterprises
Limited and Broadreach Group Ltd. He is a consultant to the
Retail Motor Industry Federation, to Trimoco plc, Sedgwick
James Ltd and Roche Products Ltd, combined with declar-
able shareholdings in Leapsquare Limited, Bradnam
Enterprises Limited and Broadreach Limited. Peter Fry, the
Wellingborough MP, has a wonderfully eclectic list: Con-
sultant to PMS Ltd., Countrywide Political Communications
Ltd and Westminster Advisers Ltd. His 'clients' include the
Bingo Association of Great Britain, South Yorkshire Passen-
ger Transport Executive, the British Leather Confederation,
Leo Burnett Ltd, Thomas Bergman and Partners, Sally Line
and Cape Industries. It's amazing that all of this activity
doesn't get in the way of his real job.

The real star of the pages of *Register of Members' Interests* is
newly elected Conservative MP for Brentford and Isleworth,
Nirj Deva, whose gobsmacking entry deserves to be reprinted
in full:

DEVA, Nirj (Brentford and Isleworth)
1. Directorships
   Parliamentary and Public Affairs International
   Ltd. (PPAI)
   Fitzroy Aviation Ltd (Director Designate).
   Ceylon and Foreign Trades Ltd. (Sri Lanka).
2. Employment of Office

Parliamentary Adviser to Turkish Cypriot
Association of the UK (April 1992).
4. Clients
Principal clients of PPAI with whom I am directly
involved:
Rothman's International.
EDS (Electronic Data Systems Corp.).
Laing International Ltd.
KHD (Great Britain) Ltd.
TECHPRO Ltd.
6. Overseas Visits
July 1992, three day visit to Copenhagen, as Joint
Secretary of Aviation Committee, paid for by
Thomson CRM.
August 1992, ten-day visit to Uganda, entertained
as state guest of the President of Uganda.
August/September, 14-day visit to Sri Lanka,
entertained as state guest of the President of Sri
Lanka.
October 1992, five-day visit to Washington D.C.,
as Joint Secretary of Aviation Committee, paid for
by British Airways.
8. Land and Property
Family interests in tea, rubber and coconut
plantations in Sri Lanka.
Distillery and residential property in Sri Lanka.
9. Declarable Shareholdings
Waulegalle Distillers Ltd. (Sri Lanka).
Erabodagama Estates Ltd. (Sri Lanka).

Register of Members' Interests on 1 December 1992. London:
HMSO, p.23.

Compared with such encyclopaedic portfolios, the much
vaunted trade union sponsorship of Labour MPs looks little
short of pathetic. Bruce George MP lists his sponsorship 'by
APEX, who contributed £600 to my 1992 election expenses',
and Roger Godsiff, the Birmingham MP, defiantly declares
that he is 'sponsored by the GMB trade union, who pay up to
80% of my election expenses'. Whilst Labour's Deputy

Leader, Margaret Beckett, has 'a room provided by the T&GWU in Derby as an office'. Now there's richness, as Dickens might have put it.

In the interests of impartiality it may be worth noting that one Tony Banks MP is a non-executive director of LBC Radio, a member of the board of the London Marathon, the Musicians' Union and the London Beekeepers' Association, and parliamentary adviser to BECTU, the broadcasting union; he also has finance for a research assistant provided by the International Fund for Animal Welfare.

Other Members have more abstruse interests to declare. Andrew Faulds MP, under 'Trades or Professions etc', describes himself as 'actor with a valuable voice', whilst Dr Liam Fox, MP for Woodspring, points out that he is a 'lecturer in emergency medicine'. The newly elected Jim Dowd MP has obviously no desire to avail himself of Dr Fox's services, putting down under the 'Financial Sponsorships, Gifts etc' category, his 'complimentary membership of the Living Well Health Club'.

Although it may be described as little short of tragic that ministers are excluded from this very agreeable financial merry-go-round, if you reach the very top, there are compensations. The Government has a small number of what are termed 'grace and favour' residences, which are put at the disposal of those at the very top of the pile.

Chevening, an exquisite country house in Kent, is generally given to the incumbent Foreign Secretary. It is widely thought that when Margaret Thatcher dumped Geoffrey Howe as her Foreign Minister, one of the bitterest pills he had to swallow was the loss of his beloved Chevening. Dorneywood in Buckinghamshire, almost as gracious, is the country abode of the Chancellor of the Exchequer and, according to Hansard (12/12/89), 'the Government own a number of other properties in London, including Admiralty House, which are used by Ministers who require them for their official duties'. The Prime

Minister, in addition to Downing Street, has Chequers, which comes in very handy for entertaining and long weekends.

The problem with all of these places is you no sooner get your feet under the table, and sort out where the hall light switches are, than you're on your way again. What you've never had, you never miss, but for those who have seen the land of milk and honey, exile is a very bitter thing, as Geoffrey Howe, Nigel Lawson and Norman Lamont could no doubt testify.

Good Times in the House of Commons

Any MP, when elected, has to face up to spending depressingly large amounts of time within the Palace of Westminster, hanging around for endless late night votes and generally trying to kill time.

The House of Commons has a large number of bars and restaurants which, when you first set foot in the place, seem very swish and exciting. Unfortunately, as with anything, familiarity breeds, if not contempt, a certain sense of *déjà vu*, and as with any works canteen, you end up thinking, 'Oh no! Not vegetarian lasagne again!' However, here is a Bonky's eye view of what the House has to offer by way of diversions when you're waiting for that 10 pm vote.

The Terrace

Only open in the summer months, and absolutely lovely when it's sunny (ie about one day in twenty). When the sun shines, the stone floor and surrounding Palace walls make the Terrace a real heat-trap. Alongside runs the Thames. Pimms is a Terrace speciality, and it is a first-class place to bring visitors or constituents on a long June evening. Good sport can be had by raising your full glass to the passing boat-loads of trippers, and greeting them with the cheery salutation, 'It's all free in here!' If they speak English, the reaction is highly satisfying.

Dining on the Terrace

Again only in summer. A long, glass-sided dining room runs down half the length of the Terrace. The view is great, and the food not at all bad. Decorated in tasteful blues and greens, it is a semi-pavilion affair, with a canvas roof. There is a help-yourself, buffet-style do, with a nice line in prawns, salmon (smoked or baked), cold pies, salads, a choice of hot main course, strawberries, fruit salad, mousse and cheese and biscuits. All in all, jolly agreeable, and as in the Terrace bar, a nice place to take guests.

The Strangers' Dining Room

Great atmosphere, but an average silver service restaurant, just off Central Lobby. Wood-panelled, candles on tables, wonderful staff and very impressive wine list at great value for money prices. A good place to impress party officials and business associates.

The Members' Dining Room

Exactly the same as the Strangers', except it's Members only. Hence you get the Tory end and the Labour end, and a lot of gossipy cliques. As Sebastian Coe has explained, it's the sort of place where the new Member will sit down and someone will come up to you and point out that you 'can't sit there – it's where X always sits'.

Churchill Grill Room (formerly the Harcourt Room)

In terms of posh, this is where it's at in the House of Commons. It's the most expensive place to eat, although the visitor will not know this, since only the hosting MP is given a menu with prices. Try to guess the most expensive dish, and watch the face as you order. In this eatery, dining MPs and guests are serenaded by a resident harpist. Some might feel as though they've taken an unexpected celestial excursion; for others the lilting strings only serve to interrupt the sweetest music of all, the sound of their own voices.

Members' Smoking Room

Only MPs allowed. Where you go to smoke, drink and read the newspapers. Very London club-like, very boring. In an adjoining room there are chess sets and writing desks, usually completely empty.

Members' Bar

Often known as 'the Kremlin', this is a bit of a hangout for diehard Labour MPs, the nearest the House gets to a pub atmosphere. Very much all-men-together, hard drinking and laddish. Guests are allowed in with a Member, but this is not a place for the faint-hearted or squeamish, and is considered by the more effete MPs to be a complete hell-hole. A place to take guests you want to under-impress.

Annie's Bar

The original Annie is long since departed, but even if you wanted to, you couldn't have a drink with her, not unless you're an MP or a lobby journalist. A small, dark and out of the way bar, which is the haunt of seasoned *habitués*. Located in the bowels of the Palace, quite close by the gents' hairdressers, in which Mr Enoch Powell, when asked how he wanted his hair cut, is reputed to have replied, 'In silence'.

Pugin Room

High-ceilinged and gracious, with beautiful views of the river. The Pugin Room serves morning coffee, afternoon tea (scones, cream and sandwiches), and then switches at 6 pm to drinks and canapés. Probably the most pleasant way of killing time in the H of C. Beloved of what might be dubbed the orchid tendency, aesthetes, dandies and those with a taste for the finer things in life.

Members' Cafeteria

Where a lot of MPs go to eat. Basic and cheerful canteen food at highly reasonable prices. Beans on toast has long been its most popular dish.

Members' Tea Room

Strictly Members only and, despite the title, serves breakfast, lunch, tea, whatever, staying open as long as the House sits. Full of tatty but comfy chairs, which are occupied by gossiping MPs. The archetypal venue for the hatching of plots; the starting post for those famous 'murmurings of backbench discontent'. MPs feel safe here. Away from staff, journos and members of the public, they can gripe away happily to their heart's content, in the sure knowledge they can be as indiscreet as they like. A favourite place for the PPSs of the Party Leaders to 'take soundings', ie find out what people are saying about the boss. Very occasionally the boss will sally forth. The frequency of these royal progresses will depend on the clubability of the Leader in question. John Smith and John Major are both reasonably affable blokes, and have made several sorties. On the other hand, Margaret Thatcher's appearance in the tea room, just prior to her departure in 1990, was a rare sighting, and a sign of panic. As in the Members' bar and eating places, MPs carve out their own party territory. For some reason the Labour Party always seem to get the worst bits.

In addition to this array of eateries and watering-holes, there are the splendiferous facilities of the House of Lords (a dodgy canteen and an equally dodgy bar); and 'refreshment facilities' of a rather better standard in No. 7 Millbank and No. 1 Parliament Street. These two buildings are owned by, and adjacent to, the House itself, and have only recently been done out and converted into MPs offices, conference rooms, libraries and research rooms. Both have cafeterias and bars open to MPs and staff, which are not at all bad, if you're looking for something that is cheap, cheerful and palatable.

How to Become Irresistible

When it comes to having a good time, sex is generally pretty high on most people's agenda, and parliamentarians are little different. However, for various reasons, MPs, sexual adventuring is usually confined to wistful imaginings, and colourful stories told in the Strangers' Bar. The occasional misdemeanour by over-amorous ministers and unfaithful political husbands plus the odd bit of sexual lunacy from the MP who's having a particularly difficult time with the male menopause, has been exhaustively documented in the newspapers. But such outbursts, entertaining as they may be, really are the exception rather than the rule. Most MPs have neither the equipment, the time nor the opportunity to indulge in wild sexual high jinks. Newly elected Stan Bonky, young, free and single, will quickly find that the kudos and glamour attached to being the people's tribune does not translate into pneumatic political groupies, willing to do literally anything for a free copy of Hansard and the chance to meet Roy Hattersley. He will also find that if he does his job properly, he will have very little time for sexual pursuit, and, anyway, he'd be too tired to do anything.

However, the news is not all bad. For the MP who is serious about sex, there is fun to be had, and the magic initials after your name do offer some advantages. For many MPs, becoming irresistible ought to be a serious uphill struggle. 90% of current MPs are male, and 90% of them are over forty. Very few Members of Parliament could be described as in any way sexy. Considering the overwhelming natural handicaps which many MPs start out with, a good number of them are markedly successful when it comes to tapping off with people. How do they do it?

Henry Kissinger (not exactly a looker himself) had a theory: 'Power,' he said, 'is the ultimate aphrodisiac.' You might think that he was just saying that to cheer himself up, but he seems to have had a point. Admittedly Stan Bonky, MP for Safe Seat, and Vice-Chair of the Backbench Social Security Committee, is some way removed from Kissinger in the power stages, but you have to remember that all things are relative.

Kissinger's theory is really the only possible explanation for why attractive young women agree to spend time with men who, to put it kindly, are in no way their physical equals.

If Stan has the time and the energy, he can use the Kissinger Factor to good effect. However, it would probably be wise to proceed with caution. Dr Ruth and Marge Proops would tell him that politics is often a cruel and lonely business, and in such a world a good marriage offers things which a quick shag can't possibly provide. Because of the hours, the pressures, and the very nature of the business, the House of Commons has far more than its share of divorce and separation. The single MP gets to come home to a lonely and silent flat in London, and at weekends to drive up to a lonely and silent house in the constituency. He or she has no one to turn to when things have gone horribly and publicly wrong (don't think of your colleagues, because you won't see them for dust); no one to celebrate with when the longed-for promotion comes through (your colleagues will be green with envy and muttering about you not being up to the job). There will be no one with whom to swap stories and no one to offer sound and trustworthy advice. That MPs are sometimes prepared to risk all this for ten minutes' (hang on, let's revise that), two minutes', frantic grinding across the desk, speaks volumes about the tragic nature of the human condition and what political commentators are apt to call 'chronic short-termism'.

The other thing to be borne in mind is that when the whole business unravels, your ex-girlfriend or wife will not just be telling her mother and friends what a bastard you are. No, if she has any desire for vengeance at all, and let's face it, after being dumped most of us are big in the desire-for-vengeance stakes, she will be talking to the *News of the World* or the *Sun* or the *Daily Mirror*. You may well be faced with the edifying knowledge that the three million people who bought the paper, plus the three million others who read the family copy, plus the six million others they told at work or school the next morning, know about your sexual preferences in minute, technicolour and deeply unflattering detail. As a further twist of the knife, these things are never over in one go. It will be a three-part serialisation, and you will face days, or weeks, of agony as your peculiarities come dribbling out, all cast in a new and possibly sinister light. As you look at the trailer in the *News of the World*, 'NEXT WEEK read how sex mad MP, Bonky, boasted that he was "INSATIABLE" and insisted in unfastening my SUSPENDERS with his TEETH', you may well reflect that it really wasn't worth it.

What Stan should do (and why is it that women never seem to need such advice?) is take a look around at his more presentable fellow MPs, see what he can do to make himself a more attractive specimen, and keep his fingers (and legs) crossed that the right person will turn up.

Too Sexy for Their Seats? The Top Ten

The following constitute living proof that it is possible to be a Member of Parliament and a physically attractive human being, and all at the same time.

Michael Portillo

Hair and eyes: brown. MP for Enfield Southgate and currently a Cabinet Minister and clearly on his way to the top, Mr Portillo is undoubtedly the sexiest member of the Government. Admittedly this is not a hotly contested position, but this boy would be a contender in any company. He has the immense good fortune to be half-Spanish, which means that he looks more like a dashing Euro-politico than the usual dreary Brit.

He has the most talked about haircut in the House of Commons, other than Mr Fabricant, and his boyish good looks have earned him great acclaim.

Peter Hain

Hair: dark and curly. Eyes: grey. MP for Neath in Wales (Labour). South African by birth, Peter achieved fame in the '60s as a result of his activities in the anti-apartheid movement and the Young Liberals. Tall, lean and distinguished, he could have walked straight off the cover of a Mills & Boon Romance and, in the true style of a romantic lead, is a bit of a maverick and occasional trouble-causer.

Virginia Bottomley

Hair: blonde. Eyes: green. MP for Surrey South West, currently a member of the Cabinet and, most famously, Secretary of State at the Department of Health. The archetypal English rose. Cool, lovely and impeccably turned out, with a sort of 'look but don't touch' coquetry. The nation stood amazed when it was revealed last year that she was a teenage mum, and that the baby was conceived before she married fellow MP, the eccentric Peter Bottomley. Is reputed to be the MP about whom most of her male colleagues fantasise, although her tendency to feature on the *Today* programme, sounding rather like a dalek in a nurse's uniform, has taken some of the gloss away.

Gordon Brown

Hair: black, luxuriant but often in need of attention. His dashing image is enhanced by the loss of one hazel brown eye in a student rugby accident. MP for Dunfermline East, and Labour's Shadow Chancellor. Dark, brooding presence with sexy Scottish brogue. Is widely acknowledged to be enormously clever and ridiculously hard working. Could probably do with losing a stone, but despite this is definitely dead attractive, and a candidate for No. 10.

Paddy Ashdown

Hair: sandy blonde. Eyes: blue/green. Liberal MP for Yeovil and Liberal Democrat Party Leader. Tough, butch and athletic. Former Royal Marine and officer in the Special Boat Squadron. He speaks Mandarin Chinese, and is reputed to have the ability to kill with his bare hands. I don't know why this should make him attractive, but somehow it does. The epitome of the square-jawed hero, stiff upper lip, stiff neck, stiff back, and who knows what else?

Harriet Harman

Hair: brown, smooth and glossy. Eyes: large, blue and limpid. MP for Peckham and Michael Portillo's opposite number. Harriet is all grace, charm and sweet reason. She is much given to Laura Ashley-type numbers and looks competent, caring, beautiful and intelligent. If she ever loses her seat, she will probably do the next series of Gold Blend coffee adverts.

Michael Heseltine

Hair: blonde, brushed back and mane-like. Eyes: steely blue. MP for Henley and President of the Board of Trade. More than six feet of thrusting machismo with ridiculously long legs. Coiled tension and sexual energy concealed beneath impeccable Savile Row tailoring. A charismatic and explosive speaking style adds to the effect. Makes the earth move on an annual basis at Tory Women's Conference.

Tony Blair

Hair: light brown. Eyes: blue. MP for Sedgefield in the North East, and Labour's spokesman on Home Affairs. Tony has probably got the nicest smile in Parliament and exudes a terrifying amount of boyish charm which,combined with a barrister's sharpness, makes a rather formidable combination. He's the sort of man people want their daughters to marry. When the Labour Party market-tested their Election Broadcasts in 1992, the approval ratings shot through the roof every time Tony's smiling face came into shot. Lesser mortals can console themselves with the knowledge that his hair is thinning rapidly. Another Labour hot shot for the top.

Sebastian Coe

Hair: black. Eyes: hazel. Newly elected Conservative MP for Falmouth and exceedingly famous Olympic athlete. Built like a whippet with staying power, Seb is lucky enough to have good bone structure and a genuinely nice personality, not a usual combination. He also smiles a lot, possibly because his teeth are white enough to play cricket in. A bit too new to be fully established as a Tory matinee idol, but definitely one to watch.

Chapter Seven

The Afterlife

Sooner or later the dreadful day will dawn when you will have to face the inevitable. You're done for. Too old, too unpopular, too out of touch, or even a terrifying mixture of all three, you are past your political sell-by date, and rapidly approaching the moment when you will become an ex-MP.

Being a Member of the House of Commons is a bit like being a Moonie – hardly anyone ever quits voluntarily. When the day comes and that pair of most precious appendages are torn bloodily and bodily from you, when the letters 'MP' are ripped away, the resultant trauma is not a pretty sight. The best cure is to stick a clean dressing over the gory wound as quickly as possible. Interestingly enough, the more elaborate and expensive the dressing, the better the recovery seems to be. Hence Baroness Chalker is relatively chipper, despite losing her seat in Wallasey in the 1992 Election. Like Lord Tebbit, Lord Merlyn Rees, Baroness Williams of Crosby (formerly Shirley), Lord Jenkins of Hillhead (formerly Roy) and Lord Howe of Aberavon (formerly Geoffrey). They may all have been de-MP'd in various ways, but when they get the ermine on they feel almost normal again.

These, however, are the fortunate few. A career in the House of Lords can truly be called an afterlife; superannuated it may be, but at least there are things to do, speeches to be made, expenses to be collected, and the pretence that what you have to say is still, in some way, important. For the bulk of MPs, the Lords remains a glittering prize, out of reach and unobtainable. Most MPs will leave the Commons feeling unwanted and rejected. They will either retire, get dumped by their party or constituency, or lose their seat. From there on, for the vast majority, it is one long journey into cold oblivion. There is no gratitude in politics. There are few more distressing sights than an ex-MP haunting the House and being roundly ignored.

Defeat – the Unkindest Cut of All

In tatty Town Halls, usually after midnight and always on a Thursday, those who are about to die will see their political life flash before their eyes, as they wait for the decision of the ungrateful electorate. The incumbent, and just about to be defeated, MP will know that nemesis is approaching. Unless the seat has been lost by an absolute whisker, several signs and portents will have quite clearly pointed to the outcome. Canvass returns and reports back from the party workers will have indicated that the vote has dropped dramatically. You will have been in the Town Hall for the past three hours, eyeing the bundles of counted votes and making your own depressing calculations. Supporters will have done the same, chatted to tellers, and come to a similar and equally dismal conclusion. When the time comes to climb up on the stage and face the music, in the form of the returning officer's announcement, you will know that it's all up.

The next few minutes will be amongst the grimmest of your life. The shiny-faced git, who has just taken all that is most precious away from you, will be grinning like someone who is about to overdose on Ecstasy. The new MP's supporters will be roaring in triumph, and you will be bracing yourself to listen to the victor's speech. During this period of utter torture and humiliation, you will have to school yourself to impassivity. Try fixing your eyes on the clock at the back of the hall and silently reciting the capitals of every EC member country and their respective prime ministers. You have to remain aloof and dignified. Tears, recriminations, threats and temper tantrums should be saved for when you get outside. Once the despicable piece of fetid lowlife who has stolen your job has finished rejoicing, it will be your turn. This sort of speech is not easy to make. So full of bile and fury that you can hardly breathe, you are now expected to thank the returning officer (yes, that's the official who has just announced that you've lost), thank the police (for picking up all their overtime), and, most bitter pill, congratulate the victor. In addition to this list of pointless platitudes, you will be expected to say something about the wonders of the constituency and its plucky inhabitants, the very same plucky inhabitants who have just switched their votes to your successor. The ungrateful snivelling bastards, you will be thinking. Fifteen years of writing to the local council about their sodding drainage problems, and this is my reward. However, you must not and will not say this. For the good of the party and, importantly, for the good of your own future career, you will be measured, generous, wise and kindly. You will then walk off the platform, say a few heartening words to the weeping party workers and go home. Once safely inside your own house, you can pour yourself a pint of whisky and get totally smashed.

It is absolutely vital at this delicate moment to have somebody with you. Somebody close to you, whom you can trust. If not your spouse, then a dear and long-standing friend. Their function is quite simple. They should make sure you are in familiar surroundings, that the room is warm and comfortable, and that you have a drink. Then this supportive being should settle back and listen to the torrent of blame and denunciation that you have been bottling up for the past ten hours. A handy check list of targets follows:

The Party Leader

'What a jerk, what a completely useless jerk. It was embarrassing. Pathetic really. Do you know what people said when I was canvassing? Do you know what they said? Do you know? Well I'll tell you. "We'd vote for you, Mr Bonky," they said. "You've been a marvellous MP, but it's that prat you've got in charge. If we vote for you, it's a vote for that lunatic to become Prime Minister." Lost us thousands of votes you know, probably tens of thousands.'

The Party Headquarters

'Couldn't run a piss-up in a brewery.' You will then go through a comprehensive list of their failures: to send up the posters you'd asked for, the badges you requested, the economic briefing, the computerised electioneering package, the leaflets for pensioners – you could go on all night and probably will. You will also make physical threats against the 'patronising little bastard' in party HQ who informed you down the telephone that Safe Seat wasn't on the list of official targets and marginals, and therefore did not qualify for a supportive visit from any of the party's big guns and campaigning stars. However, in view of what you have previously said about the Party Leader, it probably wouldn't have made any difference.

The Local Party

'A complete shambles. I mean I've never seen anything like it. I'd turn up to canvass in the morning and there'd be nobody there. All in bloody bed.' You will be enormously bitter against your agent, the party Chair and your publicity officer. Your special ire will be reserved for the cretinous party member who buggered up the target mailing and sent out twenty thousand 'women's leaflets to the constituency's sizeable Catholic population, assuring them of your trenchant support for 'free abortion on demand'. If you have reached the expansive stage you will muse philosophically about the resultant denunciations of your candidature by the local Catholic clergy the Sunday before polling day. You will curse the Pope and sing a rather slurred chorus of *The Sash My Father Wore*.

The Local Press

'Were biased. They totally were. Everybody could see it. I could have had Princess Di canvassing for me stark naked and they still wouldn't have covered it. Bastards.'

Your Spouse or Dear Friend

This is one to save till last. After you've finished ranting about almost everything else, blame them. It is completely and totally unfair, and you will regret it in the morning, but whilst you're doing it, you'll feel an awful lot better.

Retreads and Boomerangs

The House of Commons, much like Class A drugs, is deeply addictive. Once over the awful initial trauma of the loss, withdrawal symptoms start to set in. Interestingly enough, this seems to operate across the board. Research and secretarial staff who have left the House to go on to other, often better paid and more prestigious jobs, still miss the place and hanker after news and gossip. In the House of Commons you are at the centre of political events, the heady scent of power pervades the wood-panelled corridors. What's more, if you are an MP you are part of a cosseted élite, respected, deferred to, your views solicited and your opinions given weight. Many people, not surprisingly, are consumed with a desire to return. There are actually a significant number who succeed in clawing their way back. In the 1992 Parliament Gerry Malone, now MP for Winchester, was previously MP for Aberdeen South. Nick Raynsford, MP for Greenwich, was previously MP for Fulham, and Bryan Davies, MP for Oldham and Royton, was previously MP for Enfield North. In addition Bryan Gould, Margaret Beckett, Iain Sproat, Teddy Taylor and Brian Sedgemore amongst others, are all retreads, who having lost their original seats managed to pick themselves up, dust themselves down and find somewhere else. Famous figures like Michael Foot and Tony Benn have had brief spells on the outside as a result of some unforeseen electoral swing or quirk of fate.

Getting back, though, can be tough, as Bryan Davies can testify, having spent almost fourteen years between seats. It's easier if you are a really big name, or if you can find something relatively quickly. The skills you acquired as an MP – speaking in public, a broad political overview, an intuitive understanding of the important people to suck up to – will stand you in good stead, but as many would-be candidates can testify, they are not infallible. If your own party isn't keen, you can always try the approach of John 'Judas' Horam, the current Conservative MP for Orpington, who was previously SDP MP for Gateshead West (1981-3) and Labour MP for the same seat (1970-81). Truly a man for all seasons, who, not surprisingly, is not universally adored.

The World Outside

Can be a bit of a grim place. If you are a mega star, a retiring minister, or have a seat in the House of Lords, you should be all right. Offers will abound. Publishers will be eager to sign up your memoirs, which will give you a cracking chance to expose the lamentable weaknesses and misjudgements of your political colleagues, whilst at the same time revealing to the world just what a far-sighted and toweringly statesperson-like figure you really were. You may very possibly be offered a newspaper column, or a series of articles, and you can have an enjoyable time appearing on the more heavyweight news and current affairs programmes to talk about The State of the Nation. If you're Denis Healey you can do all of this *and* TV adverts for Sainsburys. These attractive options, however, are only really viable for the serious political stars. Former Party Leaders, Foreign Secretaries and the like. If you were fairly successful, if not in the very top flight, things should still be okay. There will be company boards to sit on, consultancies to take up and the odd honorary degree, all of which is perfectly agreeable.

The former luminaries of the Thatcher years are all doing very nicely thank-you. Nigel Lawson has a reported £140,000 per year from three directorships, whilst Norman Tebbit (previously Secretary of State for Trade and responsible for privatising British Telecom) is on the board of British Telecom. In a similar vein, Peter Walker, previous Energy

Secretary when British Gas was privatised, is now a director of British Gas; and Lord Young, previously at the DTI and responsible for regulating the cable and wireless industry, is now Chairman of Cable and Wireless, for which his salary is a miserable £500,000. Chris Patten has been consoled for the loss of his seat by being made Governor of Hong Kong, with a salary of approximately £184,000 tax-free, at current exchange rates.

Others have not been so lucky. Bill Molloy lost Ealing North for Labour in 1979. He signed on at the dole the next day and could be found walking down to the benefits office for months, until being made Baron Molloy of Ealing in 1981. It is hard not to feel sympathy for people who are pitched so precipitously from the top of Fortune's Wheel.

Most ex-MPs tend to find work in a connected sphere. Lobbying is a great favourite. Gerry Malone MP was an arch lobbyist during his wilderness years, and the gnomic ex-MP for Leicester East, Peter Bruinvels, who lost his seat in 1987, is spending his time as a lobbyist whilst making keen efforts to return. Graham Tope, the former Liberal MP for Sutton and Cheam, is now leader of Sutton Council. Both Margaret Beckett and Bryan Gould worked in television after losing their seats and before returning to the Commons.

Not every ex-MP is desperate to return. Every election sees its group of self-selecting retiring MPs, although some, like the former Defence Minister Alan Clark, then change their minds and try to get back. Other ex-Members find the world outside perfectly congenial and are quite happy in their new professions. Very occasionally a Member decides that he's just had enough, and leaves voluntarily to do something else. The Labour MP Stuart Holland resigned his seat in Vauxhall in 1989 and happily went off to Italy to resume his academic career. This is a rare exception to the rule. Whilst the great majority of MPs are always whinging on about how impossible the job is, very few of them would turn their grumbling into action and seek work elsewhere.

The fact is many MPs are just unemployable outside of politics, either because they have no skills worth paying for, or because if they are ex-MPs seeking work, they find it difficult to convince an employer that they won't spend all of their time trying to get re-elected.

The House of Lords – Proof of Life After Death

In terms of ex-MPdom, the House of Lords is really where it's at. You can hang round in the Palace of Westminster to your heart's content, do most of the things you used to meet your mates and talk about old times. It's a reassuringly gentle routine, sitting for only about one hundred and fifty days a year, with a style of debate characterised by a measured and lofty tone, far removed from the energetic slanging matches which frequently occur in the Commons. Although the Lords don't get paid, there is a generous attendance allowance, which means they can claim up to £97 per day (including overnight stay) and a further £29 per day for secretarial and administrative costs, which can constitute a handy supplement to the MP's pension. Naturally you don't have to do anything so undignified as clocking on or off. You just have to be there, and if you choose to spend your whole day sleeping in the Chamber, you still qualify to pick up.

There are currently almost twelve hundred members of the House of Lords, divided into Bishops, Law Lords, Hereditary Peers and Life Peers. The Bishops and Law Lords are small and rather specialised groups, who tend to keep their interventions strictly within the boundaries of their own areas. The real weight of numbers in the Lords is carried by the Hereditary Peers. There are nearly eight hundred of them, entitled to sit in the Second Chamber and legislate simply by dint of being born. Fortunately, yer actual nobility are usually much too busy shooting grouse and chasing foxes to bother themselves with running the country. These so-called 'backwoodsmen' provide the Lords with an in-built Tory majority, although it is a weapon that can only be mobilised with discretion. If there is a vote of great importance, which the Tories look like losing, their whips will get on the phone and trawl round the stately homes of England. After quite a lot of pleading, begging and persuasion, the blue bloods will clamber into the back of the Bentley and tell Jeeves to set course for Westminster. In July of 1993, when the Lords voted on the Maastricht Ratification Bill, the parliamentary car park resembled some sort of very up-market vintage car rally, as the nobles of the land responded to the Government's rallying cry to save the day. However, there is a limit as to how much you can ask from the likes of the Duke of Omnium and his gout-ridden gang, and this sort of tactic isn't reusable on too regular a basis.

Hereditary Peers are there by virtue of their ancestors having done an old king or an old queen a favour, or perhaps having purchased the peerage, when same old king or queen was in a financial hole. Life Peers get a place by doing old Prime Ministers a favour. Since 1945, ten Prime Ministers have between them created something like eight hundred peerages, both hereditary and life. Now that's a lot of favours and a lot of patronage. Who are these people? Well the *House of Commons Education Sheet Number Five* is instructive on the social background of those who sit in the Lords, and quotes from a study of two hundred and seventy Peers in the 1979-80 session of Parliament.

> The majority of Members had attended public schools. One hundred and fifty two had been to university, of whom one hundred and fourteen went to Oxford or Cambridge. Many of the others had been to Sandhurst, one of the Royal Naval Colleges or the Royal Agricultural College. The House, then as now, had a strong landowning interest as some Lords had inherited estates.

Having finished this thumbnail sketch, the author issues a strong warning: 'You should not, however, assume that Members of the House of Lords are necessarily rich.' Well, I have to say the thought had never crossed my mind.

To be made a Life Peer, you have to have clawed your way up to a level of reasonable seniority within your own particular party. If you're a real mover and shaker – Chief Whip, Home Secretary or something of the like – you will get offered a peerage almost automatically. If you are slightly lower down the scale, it will start to matter whether your Party Leader likes you or not. If they don't, then you won't get in. Simple as that. Immediately following a General Election, a sizeable number of ex-MPs will be pleading their own case to their Party Leader for a ticket to the Lords. Few will be lucky. This shuffling band of political outcasts haunts the corridors of Westminster, bending the ears of anyone who will listen to their claims for ennoblement.

Stan, on his way to the top, will have remembered that old age can be a chilly and uncomfortable affair. Faultlessly and relentlessly loyal and supportive to whomever happened to be in charge of the party, he announces his impending retirement to a relieved local constituency in Safe Seat. Having done his damnedest to ensure his successor is the candidate of his choosing, he will graciously hand over the reins and stand down in the October General Election. When the November Honours List is published he will be 'surprised and delighted' to find out that he has been made a Life Peer.

In his twilight years, Stan will dodder on his walking frame happily through the scarlet and gold corridors of their Lordships' House. He will take tea, drink House of Lords' port, and make occasional speeches about the breakdown of law and order, and the 'Need to Make Britain Great Again'. Finally, he will be called to the great Parliament in the sky. His memorial service will take place at St Margaret's, Westminster, and will be attended by two hundred and fifty of his former political colleagues, none of whom will have a bad word to say about him.

Lord Bonky of Safest Seating

From The Rt Hon. the Lord Bonky of Safest Seating
House of Lords
London SW1A 0AA

Sir & Madam

My attention has been drawn to a book entitled *Out of Order,*
which in part purports to be based upon myself. It can only be
described as an exercise in the worst kind of cynical fantasy,
and typical of those whose lack of respect for our great in-
stitutions has done so much damage to the standing of this
once proud nation.

As a Member of the greatest of all parliaments, I have served
my country and my Party for over twenty five years, without a
thought for myself, and I recognise not one word of your
highly coloured, not to say libellous, description of my former
career.

As a public servant, one does not look for praise and gratitude.
It is enough that one has served. However, I feel it is my duty
to put the record straight, and to that effect I have referred the
matter to my solicitors, Wilson Keppel and Betty, from whom
you will be hearing shortly.

Yours,

LORD BONKY OF SAFEST SEATING